Language and the Curriculum

Practitioner Research in Planning Differentiation

Deirdre Martin and Carol Miller

David Fulton Publishers

David Fulton Publishers Ltd
Ormond House, 26–27 Boswell Street, London WC1N 3JD

First published in Great Britain by David Fulton Publishers 1999

Note: The right of Deirdre Martin and Carol Miller to be identified as the authors of this work has been asserted by them in accordance with the Copyright, Designs and Patents Act 1988

Copyright © Deirdre Martin and Carol Miller 1999

British Library Cataloguing in Publication Data
A catalogue record for this book is available from the British Library

ISBN 1–85346–545–3

Typeset by Textype Typesetters, Cambridge
Printed in Great Britain by The Cromwell Press Ltd, Trowbridge, Wilts.

Contents

Preface

The final chapter of our book, *Speech and Language Difficulties in the Classroom*
presented examples of curriculum activities in which teachers had given
particular consideration to language. The language needs of the children, the
language of the adults and the language of the curriculum had been 'unpicked'
and then carefully woven into teaching and learning activities. A reviewer of the
book commented that more of these examples could usefully be made available to
practitioners. In this book, we have therefore taken further examples from the
work of practising teachers and speech and language therapists who have
reflected on the appropriateness and success of their teaching with learners who
have speech and language difficulties. The chapters focus on central issues
concerning the relationship between language, learning and the curriculum. The
practitioners chart their cycle of planning, teaching, evaluating, planning and
teaching again. They discuss their perceptions and reflections on the effectiveness
of their teaching and the children's learning.

The meticulous way in which the practitioners plan their work, taking account
of children's individual needs, is striking. No less impressive are the reflections
and self-evaluation which lead to further developments in their teaching and in
the children's learning. Language is the primary tool for teaching and learning in
the majority of settings and we hope that the examples in this book will provide a
framework for other practitioners, working with a range of abilities and needs in
the classroom.

The chapters could not have been written without the help of a number of
colleagues. They contributed their examples and allowed us to adapt them for this
present purpose. We are extremely grateful to the following people for generously
providing material and ideas for the chapters which follow: Ruth Afako, John
Belfield, Sue Bond, Heather Brooker, Michael Clegg-Butt, Mary Gambrill, June
Green, Andrea Kreyenborg-Nichols, Alison Marshman, Patience Skilling.

Deirdre Martin and Carol Miller
Birmingham
November 1998

Chapter 1

Language, learning and the curriculum

Introduction

Language is central to learning. It provides the main tool for teaching and learning and, by experiencing language for these purposes, children's language develops further. Through active participation and through interaction with people and with their environment, children learn to make sense of their world. Learning and, in particular, learning through the use of language, is an intellectual, emotional and social activity. In this chapter, we look at some of the ways of understanding the relationship between language and learning. We also consider some of the implications for children whose language does not develop easily and therefore does not provide them with an automatic tool for learning.

The curriculum is the focus for learning in school and in the chapters which follow, teachers' and speech and language therapists' work shows how pupils with speech and language difficulties are supported in their learning to access and achieve curriculum targets. They discuss language, not only as it is used for specialist subject and topic-based learning, but also as it is used for learning about how to approach learning tasks, how to behave in a group and how to negotiate needs. The chapters thus explore aspects of language and learning in the classroom taking account of curriculum, context and tasks for language and learning development.

The teachers and therapists in the chapters show, through their teaching, their beliefs about how children learn, how language develops and how speech and language difficulties influence learning. Further, since practitioners are also learners, they reflect on their own ways of learning and how these influence the way they work with children and with colleagues. One of the aims of this chapter is to encourage practitioners to reflect on the approach they have to children's learning and language and the extent to which this motivates and influences their teaching and evaluation.

Language and cognition

The relationship between language and learning is complex and not fully understood. A widely held view is that language is a specialised domain of cognitive functions and that similar, but distinct, processes are involved in learning language and in other forms of learning. It is important that practitioners working with learners with language difficulties understand the possible relationships between language and cognition since this group of learners has difficulties in one or both of these systems. The cognitive system which makes learning operational can be considered to have a number of features (Dockrell and McShane 1993). *Memory* is an important aspect of learning and is usually considered to comprise short-term memory, also known as working memory, which passes information to long-term memory through techniques such as repetition and practice. The information or knowledge base in the memory is stored as *mental representations* The strategies to access the knowledge base and mental representations are known as *task processes,* which are controlled by *executive processes.* These are thought to give rise to knowledge about one's own learning, so-called *metacognitive* knowledge.

Areas of knowledge, such as reading or mathematics, are called 'domains' and it is hypothesised that language is an autonomous cognitive domain (Fodor 1983, Ellis and Young 1988). That is, language has similar but distinct structures and processes to other cognitive domains and linguistic information is processed through innate central language-specific structures. There is a memory component which stores linguistic representations, such a speech sounds, words and larger lexical units and phrases. The representations and knowledge base about language are accessed by task processes controlled by metalinguistic knowledge, that is, executive processes.

Practitioners can refer to this approach to help understand the relationship between language and learning in their practice. The approach may be helpful in understanding pupils' difficulties as these can sometimes be identified as particular problems with memory or in accessing information from the mental representation. Particular assessment tasks can be used to examine these aspects and activities can be designed to encourage development or to compensate their inadequacies.

Approaches which bring together cognitive and language processing are called *psycholinguistic* models because of the ways in which they use information from cognitive psychology and from linguistics. Stackhouse and Wells (1997) have proposed a psycholinguistic model which links phonological and literacy development. The model attempts to show relationships between different levels of processing speech sounds in words and relationships with the written form of words. Difficulties in listening to, or producing speech sounds in words, as well

2

as reading, spelling and writing words are identified as difficulties in processing at different levels in the model. This model offers practitioners a systematic approach to assessment and intervention with individuals who have speech and literacy difficulties.

For example, a child may fail to develop a distinction between particular speech sounds, such as 't' and 'k' so that she says:

'tan I have a tup of tea' for 'can I have a cup of tea'.

She is also likely to have difficulties in reading, writing and spelling words with these speech sounds because she has faulty lexical representations and/or has difficulties processing specific speech information.

Describing language

When working with learners who have speech and language difficulties it is important that practitioners are familiar with ways of describing language. They need 'a language to talk about language' if they are to identify the particular strengths and needs of individual children. As Crystal points out:

it is of course impossible to do without theoretical or descriptive terms in even the most casual analysis of language. (Crystal 1987, p. 82)

There are a number of ways of describing language and they vary in their linguistic technicality and in their approach to language. For example, language can be analysed and described grammatically, looking at the structure of elements of words and sentences. Examples of this approach are offered by Graddol, Cheshire and Swann (1994). Alternatively, the function of different aspects of grammar can be described, as given by Jackson (1990). There are also descriptions of language according to its use, as suggested by McTear (1985). The various ways of describing language give attention to *form* and *function* at surface level, that is, language performance.

Form and function

Language can be seen as a complex system in which different aspects or levels interact. Most importantly, there is interaction between form and function, where form is the structure of language, and function concerns how language is used (Pinker 1994). There is a close relationship between form and function and constructing well-formed utterances is crucial for making meaning. The structure of sentences, words and speech sounds is generated by a system of rules which vary from language to language.

3

At sentence level English has rules about word order so that the meaning of the sentence changes if the order of the words changes. At word level there are rules about word endings (morphology), such as plurals, tense, comparison, and in some languages, case endings. Also at word level there are rules which determine whether a word is a noun, an adjective, an adverb or a verb and there are rules for prefixes and suffixes. Further, there are rules which link words with similar roots, such as 'know' and 'knowledge'; 'flower', 'floral' and 'florist'. Finally, there are rules which determine the organisation and meaningful contrasts of speech sounds in words (phonology), so that *bap, cap, lap* have different meanings, as have *pin, pit, pig,* although each group of words is similar in their speech sounds.

Using language to make meaning brings variation to grammar rules. There are always attempts to describe and then prescribe the rules of a language to obtain a 'standard form'. Standard forms are helpful but are likely to change because language is dynamic. Today's standard form may be tomorrow's dialect. In the chapters of this book, some of the practitioners note the tension between the national curriculum requirement in assessment for standard forms of English and the efforts of learners to make meaning, despite their difficulties with language form.

The other main approach to understanding language is through its functions, that is, how it is used. It is often referred to as *pragmatics* and is a more recent area of language study. In a cognitive framework, language use is explained by involving processes not only in the language domain but also in the social domain. It concerns the 'rules governing the use of language in context' (Bates 1976), that is, matching context and communication with the grammatical form of the utterance. A comprehensive definition given by Foster (1990) describes pragmatics thus:

> Among other things, it includes how speakers use utterances to make requests, promises and threats; how utterances differ in the degree to which they are polite; how the structure of the utterances allows speakers to background some information while foregrounding other information. In fact it covers all the ways in which grammar serves the needs of speakers as social human beings. (Foster 1990, pp. 6–7)

The example which is often taken to illustrate the importance of form influencing meaning, concerns the active and passive forms:

1. Beavers build dams
2. Dams are built by beavers
(Pinker 1994, p. 122)

Speakers choose the active form in (1) to focus meaning on *beavers* and the passive form in (2) to emphasise *dams.* Another important feature is that although the meaning between the two sentences is similar, the difference in form has altered the meaning. (2) is not accurate because dams are not built exclusively by beavers.

The relationship between form and function has implications for working on language development with children with language difficulties. The pragmatics of language is particularly important for several reasons. It is a basis for very early communication since it precedes speech and language. Later on it assists generalisation of grammatical structures. It is important for successful social development as well as building up communicative confidence and assertiveness in children with communication difficulties. Improving pragmatic language skills can also help prevent problems in later educational performance (Andersen-Wood and Smith 1997, pp. 2–3).

There are several reasons why it is important to be able to describe language and many of them are evident in the accounts of practitioners' work in this book. It is important to be able to have a means of talking about language. As children develop knowledge about language (sometimes referred to as 'KAL'), both they and their teachers require a vocabulary which describes their observations about language. Children may not need to be familiar with the details of parsing and types of clauses but it can be useful to know about the idea of a sentence and different sentence types, such as questions, requests and exclamations, and the ways we use them. There may be many other occasions, both planned and spontaneous, when being able to label a phenomenon, such as rhyming, rhythm, plurals, verb tenses, irony, may help children to understand the characteristics of spoken and written language. More importantly, practitioners working with children who have special needs in speech and language, will want to identify the aspects of language form and function. Without this, it will be difficult to know which aspects of language to assist, for example where children are developing English as an additional language or who have specific language difficulties. Using descriptions of language entails not only noting features of the children's language but also identifying modifications which need to be implemented in the practitioners' language and in curriculum language, in order to make language for learning accessible to the children. Further, teachers and speech and language therapists, the practitioners who work together in this field, need to be familiar with each other's ways of describing language so that they can communicate effectively with each other in discussion of children's language needs.

Descriptions of language do not seek to explain the processes behind performance as described in the section above on cognition and language. Both linguistic description and identification of features of language processing can be useful in working with children's language.

Sequence of language development

Due largely to the work of Lenneberg (1967) it is widely accepted that the brain has a biological predisposition for learning language, which develops through maturation. That is, it follows predetermined stages, in a similar way to other aspects of human development. A great deal of empirical work showed that emerging language in children seemed to follow similar sequences in first language English (see for example, Brown 1973) and in second language English (for example, Krashen 1982). These studies focused on the emergence of morphemes, such as plurals, verb endings and some prepositions. However, subsequent studies which looked at other aspects of emerging language found more individual variation, both in first language English (Wells 1985) and in second language English (for example, Skehan 1998). These findings may well coincide with the experiences of practitioners. Wells' study in particular produced so much data on language development that it was possible to challenge the notion of age-stage language development. They found that children who were functioning similarly in expressive language could have age differences of up to 24 months. This finding was referred to as the 'Universal Fallacy' (Richards 1995) and it challenges the notion of 'universal' language development of age-stage checklist.

These observations suggest that practitioners need to be more aware of individual developmental differences in their assessment and teaching. The classroom practitioner has to marry the uniqueness of individual differences in language development, particularly among those with language difficulties, with group commonalities. In order to provide the entitlement of curriculum learning, the practitioner must meet the individual needs of this group of language learners while working within the broad bands of acknowledged stages of language development. Variations in individuals developing language may be due to a variety of reasons. For example, their development will be influenced by their genetic endowment or their environment and how they interact with it according to their age, gender, culture, and personality. This is taken up again later in the chapter.

Language difficulties

Each child learns language in their own way and in their own time. In some cases children show unusual delay in achieving certain stages and aspects of language. Fortunately, most of these children 'catch up' and their language no longer seems delayed in comparison with their peers. Often this delay is resolved before or during the early years of schooling. For other children however, language develops in a noticeably unusual way, which may continue to cause concern, even with intervention and language support. These are the children we are concerned with here.

Substantial language difficulties are often explained as difficulties in cognitive processing and consequently, teaching and intervention strategies are orientated to develop and improve processing. For example, difficulties in language comprehension may be interpreted as difficulties in auditory processing. This would lead to more time being allowed for processing auditory verbal input, emphasising listening and auditory discrimination work. Difficulty with understanding or using the correct order of words may lead to work on auditory sequential skills, such as following instructions, sequencing activities and emphasis on temporal aspects of language such as adverbs of time and verb tenses. Language difficulties may be understood to be due to constraints in working memory which impair recall of words or structures. This may result in working directly on the child's ability to pay attention and concentrate. Recently, phonological and literacy difficulties have been interpreted as difficulties in developing and accessing phonological representations. Thus, intervention has emphasised enhancing, recalling and using sound patterns of language.

There are other hypotheses offered to explain language difficulties. For example, generalised cognitive learning difficulties may include the language-specific domain. Children may have difficulties with hierarchical organisation, which includes the hierarchical organisation of language structures (e.g. Cromer 1991). This is evident when children understand and use linear utterances, as in (a), but are unable to handle *embedding*, when a phrase is inserted into the main sentence, as in (b):

(a) the boy and girl are running
(b) the boy but not the girl is running.

Other hypotheses explain language difficulties as difficulties with symbol representation, that is in understanding that one thing can represent another (Bishop and Mogford 1988, Bruner 1981). This would be manifest in other levels of symbolic representation, such as literacy and numeracy.

Studies of families with high prevalence of language difficulties suggest that there are genetic predispositions for language difficulty and links with gender (Pembry 1992). This may partly explain the long-observed higher incidence of language difficulty among boys. Other studies suggest that in the absence of cognitive and other sensory, physical and social difficulties, some children can experience particular rule-making difficulties in language, that is they may have specific language impairment (SL1) (Van Der Lely 1997). They demonstrate substantial, long-term difficulties in understanding and in developing linguistic aspects of communication. Further, there are studies which show that there are children who demonstrate a disjuncture between form and function, so that they develop rule-making skills and memory skills but have difficulties using language communicatively in context (Smith and Leinonen 1992).

In the chapters which follow many of the children have other difficulties in addition to language problems. Some children have generalised cognitive difficulties which show in slower maturational development in learning. Others have emotional and behaviour difficulties which may be linked with their problems in communication. Other children again have difficulties developing social skills which is also reflected in their functional use of language. The practitioners working with these learners reflect on ways to address not only the children's language difficulties but also other learning needs.

It is not possible in this short chapter to go into all of the possible reasons for, or manifestations of, language and communication difficulties. The field is vast and there are still many unknowns. For further information, readers may like to look at Adams *et al.* 1997, Crystal and Varley 1993, Martin and Miller 1996.

Language, cognition and intervention

The relationship between language and cognition is important for intervention. When a child's language is analysed and there appear to be difficulties in rule-making strategies at grammatical and phonological levels, cognitive approaches can be effective. Such approaches will build on metacognition and on developing cognitive awareness of language strengths and difficulties. A programme such as Metaphon (Howell and Dean 1994) for example, approaches phonological difficulties by making children aware of different features of speech sounds and the role that they play in language. Thus, games will focus on how sounds are similar and different, whether they are 'long' or 'short', 'loud' or 'quiet', so that a child becomes more aware of sounds in other people's language and in their own. The Social Use of Language Programme (Rinaldi 1995) also adopts a metacognitive approach to help learners who have difficulties with the paralinguistic features of communication, such as eye contact, volume and speed of talking. However, while these programmes are helpful to learners with language difficulties, there are also important drawbacks. These programmes operate outside the curriculum. They are focused on learners' language difficulties and are not related to other learning skills or knowledge. It would take careful planning to apply these programmes to support curriculum learning.

Social interactionist approaches to learning

A social interactionist approach to learning proposes that learning happens through interaction between the learner and 'significant others'. These significant others may be adults or peers who know more, or who have more skills than the learner and who select and shape experiences for the learner. Through social interaction these important people, *mediators*, move learners from their current level of knowledge to the next level or layer. This was termed the learner's *zone of proximal development* (ZPD) by Vygotsky (1962) and it indicates the difference between what the learner can do and what the significant other is trying to encourage them to do. The notion of mediation and ZPD has been developed by others as a theory of learning (Rogoff and Wertsch 1984) and in recent years has gained more prominence in school-based teaching and learning. Thus, learning is not centred in one person, teacher or learner, but rather in the act of mediation. Learning is in interaction and therefore Vygotsky argued that the role of language is central to learning. Language makes sense of our experiences and is a 'tool' for learning. It operates, like thought, at a symbolic level. In social interaction, the mediator and the learner use language to negotiate the meaning of the experience. The implications for teaching are that learning does not happen by osmosis. Careful assessment and selection of appropriate tasks, social interaction and language can move the learner through the ZPD to the next layer of knowledge or skill. Further, teaching and learning which happens through social interaction can be mediated by knowledgeable others who may be teachers, parents or peers.

Learning through social interaction and mediation has also been central to Feuerstein's approach (Feuerstein *et al.* 1980). One of his basic notions is the 'principle of belief in positive outcomes'. Regardless of age or disability, all individuals can learn with appropriate tasks, social interaction and mediation within the ZPD. His theory is based on several components and a central one is the notion of *structural cognitive modifiability*. That is, individuals continue to modify their cognitive structures and develop their cognitive capacity throughout their lives. Feuerstein also uses the term 'mediation' which he has developed into a theory with three essential features:

- the significance and value of what is being learnt must be understood by teacher and learner;
- the purpose and relevance of the learning experience must be perceived beyond the immediate needs, and
- the intention of the task must be clearly presented by the teacher and understood by the learners.

Both Vygotsky and Feuerstein emphasise the importance of the social context in learning. In addition, individuals bring to learning their own personal characteristics, such as age, gender, personality, feelings, self-concept, motivation, experience and cultural background. Learning is processed through the cognitive system and needs to be developmentally appropriate. It is most effective when it is personally relevant to the learner and proceeds through authentic experience. New knowledge needs to be mediated by others through interaction and individuals learn in their own unique way with adults and peers. In the chapters which follow, there are examples which show practitioners' detailed awareness of children's individual characteristics. The activities described show how the social context and the interactions are integral to the children's learning.

The curriculum, context and task analysis

This last section deals with the main demands on the practitioner in meeting the children's language needs through the curriculum, creating an environment and structured opportunities in which to learn language and knowledge, to develop language-conscious tasks for teaching the curriculum and to consider approaches to evaluating learning. We have suggested above that children learn from active participation in their learning and that language is not separate from learning but a 'tool' for learning. The implications for the curriculum are that language learning is not a separate learning dimension but should be integral to other learning. The challenge for practitioners working with learners with speech and language difficulties is to develop contexts and tasks which enable learning through language which is appropriate and supportive to their diverse needs. Additionally, these tasks will also promote the further development of language.

Context

The context for learning language includes both the physical environment and the structured opportunities to learn language. It is true that the physical environment for all learners should be supportive to their needs, providing a context where they feel secure, confident and willing to take risks but this has particular significance where children have communication difficulties. Often small, specialised classes can achieve this. Large, mainstream classrooms can be intimidating for children with speech and language difficulties and particular care may be needed to protect their dignity and self-esteem.

Collaboration between practitioners in planning and working together is essential, particularly for learners with speech and language difficulties. Class or subject teachers, support teachers, classroom assistants and speech and language therapists need to pool their expertise in joint lesson planning.

The organisation of the classroom is an important factor in the learning context, and again, may be particularly necessary for children with language difficulties. There needs to be both learning and talking space for problem-solving and interaction with peers as well as one-to-one interaction with an adult. Teachers group children for selected learning and language purposes, such as whole or half class activities, small groups for collaborative work, paired or individual study and working with other classes. Careful consideration needs to go into the formation and purpose of these groups. In the chapters which follow, there are examples of the meticulous way in which teachers do this to maximise learning opportunities for the children and, indeed for themselves.

In the management of learning with a class of children with language difficulties it is important to create a curriculum of equality, where learners are given a 'voice' to talk about and listen to each others' perspectives on different issues about difference and disability. It is important to create these opportunities within the class group to facilitate learning at both cognitive and affective levels. Establishing this feature of the curriculum will be particularly important for learners with language difficulties if they are to be included in mainstream schooling.

Structured language opportunities

Young childen are surrounded by language. They learn language at home from interested adults and siblings, as well as at school. However, there are important differences between the language of home and school. At home, language is used primarily for communication and most learning is incidental, informal and not prominent. By contrast, in school and other formal educational settings, language is used for learning, when it is focused and selected and designed for learning, as in lesson time. Teachers and other classroom practitioners need to plan structured language learning opportunities in order to maximise learning, not only for all learners but even more so for learners with language difficulties.

In addition to the use of language for learning, there is also a social purpose for language in the classroom. Teachers and learners use language for social control, such as in requests for information and permission. Language is used for negotiating, for assertion and denial, for rule-making and decision-making, as well as for humour and the expression of emotions. Children with language difficulties need to be taught these aspects of language use just as much as they need to be taught the language of the curriculum and how to use language for learning. In the chapters which follow, there are examples where planning has included this aspect of classroom language.

Language for learning in the curriculum requires a level of consciousness to be created for the learner and also for the teacher. That is, both the adults and the children in the classroom need to be conscious of their language behaviour. In the earlier discussions of learning, it is clear that an awareness of learning and a consciousness of how old knowledge is being extended and reorganised, enables learners not only to learn in that situation, but also to transfer learning to other situations. It is equally important that there is a similar consciousness of language learning. This is central to learning for children with language difficulties.

Earlier the importance of knowledge about language (KAL) and its implications for developing metalinguistic knowledge in children, was discussed. However, there is a need to go beyond KAL for learners with language difficulties, to support their language and learning needs in the curriculum. For example, this group of learners usually have problems developing vocabulary. One strategy to support their vocabulary acquisition is to raise their awareness of the relationships between words in curriculum learning. These learners need to have their attention drawn to similarity and oppositeness between word meanings (synonymy and antonymy). They need to be made aware of words which go together and how groups of words can be classified. They need to have attention drawn to word roots, suffixes and prefixes (morphology). As an example, take the science curriculum topic of sinking and floating. The teacher and therapist could encourage:

- thinking of synonyms for 'floating' and 'sinking';
- identifying features of oppositeness of 'sink' and 'float';
- noting that the verbs 'sink' and 'float' have other meanings as nouns;
- thinking of words which go together with 'sink' and 'float', such as sink-bottom and float-top;
- grouping and categorising words which can 'sink' and 'float' such as stone, cork, stick;
- paying attention to the grammatical features of the two words: that they are action words, they form tenses and participles;
- raising phonological awareness of the words, through beating them out syllabically, listening to sounds of alliteration and rhyme, and talking about sounds at the beginnings and ends of words and parts of words.

Practitioners' use of language

There is also the practitioners' consciousness, not only of the children's language, but possibly more importantly, of their own use of language. There are several examples in the chapters where the teachers and therapists are aware of their use of language as a potential contributing factor to the children's difficulty in accessing the curriculum.

Many children with language difficulties can only understand and use language in a literal sense. They would be confused by expressions such as 'floating an idea', 'floating on the breeze' or 'a sinking feeling' because of the abstract meaning. Adult language is full of these types of expressions and more. There are similes, 'as good as gold'; metaphors, 'she's golden'; phrasal verbs, 'get by' (meaning to manage), 'turn down' (reject). Teachers' use of non-literal, metaphorical language may need particular attention. We cannot refrain from using these phrases, indeed, they are an essential part of the richness and diversity of the English language. However, we need to become aware of them and use them judiciously. They can become a focus for learning, where their meaning can be unpicked and understood (Marshmán, in press). Older learners can be encouraged to use a dictionary and thesaurus to identify meanings.

It is a feature of many classrooms that teacher interaction with pupils is still largely directed by the adult and that many teachers' questions to pupils are not 'genuine' (Morgan and Saxton 1991). That is, questioning is used to maintain control or as an assessment, to see whether children can recall something, rather than a tool for mutual problem-solving or discovery. A more useful pedagogy encourages pupil-generated questions and increases learning with peers. This aim reflects a belief that learners with language difficulties can negotiate their learning through language and their experience. The chapters which follow offer examples of how this can be realised.

Two main approaches to developing interactive learning are through practitioner-led strategies and through peer-led strategies, and it is important to keep a balance between the two. Understanding how to use questions is a basis for developing teacher-led interaction. Questions, when used effectively, can develop a range of learners' thinking skills. Morgan and Saxton (1991) give examples of the way teachers can use questions to focus on particular aspects of children's learning, in order to develop their thinking skills.

The framework is based on Bloom's taxonomy (Bloom and Krathwohl 1965): *knowledge, comprehension, application, analysis, synthesis* and *evaluation*. For example, looking at a picture of a city scene just after a robbery, the practitioner could ask a range of questions to stimulate the learner to think in different ways (see Figure 1.1).

Practitioners working with learners with language difficulties could also use these questions for assessing which thinking skills the children found easier and more difficult in order to influence future planning and teaching. For example, difficulty with Question 1 may lead to vocabulary work and matching activities, while difficulties with Question 4 would lead to work on event relationships, such as cause and effect.

This example also illustrates that there are questions which retain control and learning with the practitioner and other questions which offer the learner the key to open themselves to the interaction and show their understanding and perspective. It is in these revelations that practitioners can become the 'significant others' and lead learners on to the next layer of knowledge, in the Vygotskian sense. In this interaction there needs to be a genuineness in communication. Practitioners' interest in the learners' communication and learning is a strong motivator for pupils to learn. In the chapters in this book there are examples of these interactions, which show the differing levels of success achieved between teachers and learners with language difficulties.

Peer-led interactions rely on practitioners constructing activities and tasks which support interactive learning: for example, creating 'information gap' tasks

13

Questions and Thinking skills

Question 1: Checking knowledge:
      What can you see in this picture?
Question 2: Comprehension:
      What do we call a place like that?
Question 3: Application:
      Do you know any other places which look like this picture?
Question 4: Analysis:
      Why are there so many policemen in this picture?
Question 5: Synthesis:
      What if there were no policemen?
Question 6: Evaluation
      Would you like to live in city like that or in a village?

(from Morgan and Saxton 1991, p. 10)

Figure 1.1

where each participant must share her/his information in order to solve the problem. Alternatively, with limited information the members of the group have to reason and make deductions in order to complete the pattern, sequence or story. Another strategy at a higher level is to problem-solve through group discussion. It is important that the learners know the ground rules of working together, which may be an achievement in itself for some learners with language difficulties, as some of the examples in the chapters illustrate.

An important aspect of successful peer-led interaction is learners' understanding of what they must do. Without this understanding, loss of interest or confusion may result. There needs to be clear and effective presentation of key components of the task, such as vocabulary, grammatical constructions and equipment. The presentation of learning tasks must also include pointing out the purpose and relevance of the tasks to the pupils, preferably related to their own lives. Their curiosity for doing the task needs to be aroused. Further, tasks may be more successful if pupils understand the task and set their own goals for doing the task and identify the means by which they will know they have achieved it. This may mean some kind of self-evaluation. It may also be necessary to link this activity with a later, extension activity, such as a video on the topic, or a visit.

Task analysis: components

Successful learning lies in identifying the learners' ZPD and moving learners on to the next layer of knowledge. There is more likelihood of optimal performance when tasks, and their component sub-tasks, are based on learners' existing skills. The content of the task is usually determined by the curriculum, but the nature of the task, as discussed above, can be constructed according to common aspects of children's abilities and differentiated according to the individual learner's needs.

For children with language difficulties, tasks need to be developed along two dimensions: contextual support and cognitive demand (Cummins 1984). That is, tasks have sufficiently rich contexts for learners to understand the demands within their language skills so that they can progress to more cognitively-demanding tasks. Learners with language difficulties can progress clockwise (see Figure 1.2) from contextually-supported tasks with low cognitive demands where language is introduced in a structured way, to activities where learning is more cognitively-demanding and more reliant on language. Within these two dimensions, tasks need to be sufficiently challenging for learners with language difficulties to learn new language and new knowledge. An example is set out in Figure 1.2.

The example concerns differentiating teaching/learning about the value of coins by moving from tasks which have low cognitive demand and much contextual support through to tasks which have higher cognitive demand, less contextual support and rely more on language for understanding and executing. Starting in the lower half of Figure 1.2, with tasks which have 'low cognitive demand', the lower left quadrant introduces knowledge of coins with substantial contextual support. Moving to the upper left quadrant, the contextual support is maintained and the cognitive demand increases with tasks which require categorising and application. In the upper right quadrant tasks which require analysis, synthesis and evaluation do not need coins. They rely on language. The lower right quadrant has an example of recognised 'time filler' activities. They have little function in learning about the value of coins but are enjoyable activities.

The importance of planning tasks and activities is evident and information obtained from evaluating learners' progress through tasks is a key to further planning.

Assessment and evaluation

For learning to take place in the case of children with difficulties, assessment and intervention need to be part of a cyclical process, of teach–check–teach. This cycle is discussed in the next chapter and, in the chapters which follow, the

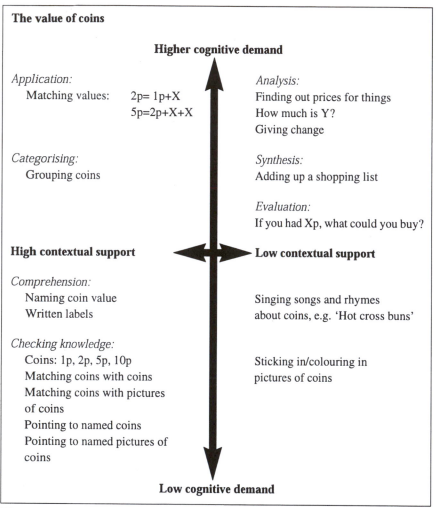

Figure 1.2

practitioners demonstrate how the essential cyclical nature of their curriculum work moves children on to further stages of development.

There are a number of different ways of assessing learning. In the chapters which follow there is little mention of formal or standardised assessment. The focus is on evaluation of learning in the curriculum which is illustrated through two approaches, by the practitioners' self-informing, cyclical teach–check–teach process and through self-assessment by the learners themselves.

Standardised and formal assessments are often used to assess learners' speech and language difficulties and their learning abilities at identified stages in the school year. Their purpose is to profile the children's skills in order to inform long-term planning for the learners in the coming academic year. By contrast, short-term and immediate teaching planning must be informed by reviewing recent achievements of learners. The evaluation of learners' performance on previous learning and language tasks informs the planning for teaching the next session.

The assessment of children's achievements will be based on three important considerations. Firstly, the assessment of language learning and knowledge learning needs to be distinguished, particularly with learners who have speech and language difficulties. The oral or written language skills of these children is unlikely to reflect accurately their knowledge. For example, pupils with difficulties in comprehension or those with auditory memory difficulties, may need more time to demonstrate their knowledge, or they may need additional visual support to understand what is required of them. In the case of some children with pragmatic difficulties, their expressive language may not relate to their knowledge. Also, learners with expressive language difficulties, such as word-finding problems, difficulties with speech sounds or in making sentences, may need to demonstrate their knowledge learning in a non-verbal way. They may demonstrate their knowledge by using flash cards or selecting written sentences.

Secondly, practitioners need to prepare learners for evaluation. They need to ensure that children understand and can be involved in the evaluation of their own learning. For example, when presenting a task to children, they can be made aware that they will be expected to draw a picture, make a model, complete a written text or a worksheet. It may be necessary to present visually, through diagrams or pictures, the sequence of events which the learners need to follow in order to successfully complete the task and the evaluation. Whenever possible, children can be encouraged to discuss and negotiate their form of evaluation. For those with speech and language difficulties this is particularly important in encouraging them to take control of their own communication.

Thirdly, effective observation and monitoring skills will enable practitioners to watch and listen to the children in their class and to notice and record their 'moments of achievement and enlightenment' (Gravelle 1996, p. 48). However, in order to do this, time and space will need to be arranged in the teaching and learning session. Ways and means of recording the evaluations of pupils' learning will develop within the overall planning scheme. This will enable practitioners to make meaningful, detailed and efficient evaluations of each learners' achievements, difficulties and learning progress.

In the chapters which follow, there are examples of practitioners' work illustrating these aspects of evaluating pupils' learning. Their own learning of the process, their identification of the difficulties and the solutions they found are apparent. Furthermore, there are examples of how practitioners encourage self-assessment by the pupils themselves. The chapters also illustrate how the practitioners used the evaluations of pupils' progress in language and knowledge learning to inform and develop the next teaching and learning sessions.

There are examples in later chapters of this book of practitioners' experiences of learner assessment. Assessment of their own performance by children is beginning to be recognised as a powerful tool for developing understanding of their own learning and the learning of others, as well as raising awareness of how they might control their own learning. Self-assessment of learning should begin with negotiating with the learners how they could evaluate their efforts at the end of a learning task. Initially, perhaps the practitioner may present only one way that pupils may present their own achievements and as they try different ways of reporting their progress they can select the way that they prefer or is most appropriate. For example, learners may discuss their achievements in a 'conference'-type format, where they present their work, outcomes and reflections to their peers in a group. For learners with language difficulties this may be a demanding procedure. They may prefer to develop non-verbal or language-supported presentations, such as displaying pictures of their work, or photographs of themselves or their partner working at different stages of the task. Completing a questionnaire or a chart showing stages of task progression may be a method appropriate for ongoing progress monitoring over several sessions. For some pupils with difficulties in presentation skills, making a tape recording of their progress may be preferable. Children can also play back and correct the assessment report, with support from the teacher or peer partner. Children can interview each other as a form of assessment which can be undertaken in front of the group or may be taped. Tape recordings and videos can also be used as a temporary or permanent record of talk, language and communication behaviour.

It is worth bearing in mind that direct questioning of pupils may not be an effective strategy for evaluating their learning. Direct questioning about knowledge is an assertive and possibly threatening approach to many pupils. It can arouse feelings of fear due to not understanding the question, not knowing the answer or being unable to admit confusion. Furthermore, pupils may supply the 'right answer' but not necessarily have the associated understanding, which can often be the case with children with language difficulties. Pupils with language difficulties may not understand certain forms of questioning, which should be known to the practitioner through prior language assessment information; they may be unable to respond in the focused way required due to interactional difficulties, word-finding difficulties or other aspects of their communication difficulty. For all these reasons it is worth exploring alternative and more empowering ways of evaluating learners' progress in language and knowledge learning.

Conclusions

Language operates through a rule-based and a memory-based system. It has formal constraints which must be recognised. Children with language difficulties can have difficulties with any and all language levels: rules, memory, and use. Further, they may demonstrate these difficulties in all aspects of language or specifically in one, such as grammar, vocabulary or phonology. Whilst for most children it can be assumed that in school they can understand and use language to learn, this assumption cannot be made where children have language and other learning difficulties. These children need particular help in gaining access to the curriculum through language. Further, the curriculum will be an important vehicle through which they will develop their language and communication skills. In the next chapter, we will look at the processes used by practitioners to develop their skills in planning, managing and evaluating the curriculum for children with language and communication difficulties.

Chapter 2

Reflecting on curriculum planning

Introduction

In Chapter 1 we considered the nature of language and how it is integral to learning. It is clear that when children have difficulties with language, or with other areas of learning, then special considerations will be needed for their education. Practitioners who work with them will need particular knowledge and skills. In addition to understanding the curriculum and subjects within it, these practitioners will be especially aware of the nature of language. They will need skills in identifying where language and curriculum are linked so that they can support children, through language, in gaining access to the curriculum. Additionally, they will know how to develop children's language and communication through the curriculum. In this chapter, we look at an approach to curriculum management which forms the basis for examples in subsequent chapters.

The desire to learn is an essential characteristic of professionalism and one of the characteristics of a professional is:

> one who continually seeks mastery of the branch of learning on which his (sic) occupation is based. (Jarvis 1983, p. 27)

Professional development can result from any activity which enhances the knowledge and skills of practitioners and keeps them up-to-date and active in their professional role. It comes not only from formal courses but from a whole range of opportunities undertaken alone or with colleagues. Reading a book, a report, or a journal article for example, would be important ways of informing oneself and gaining new ideas; a discussion group or a special interest group may be set up to explore a particular aspect of practice; individual colleagues may present case studies or experiences of their work and invite others to comment and discuss them. Opportunities to share ideas with colleagues and to learn from each other are important:

> the most effective staff development occurs when teachers are helping one another to reflect on their own practices. (Wheal 1995)

In this chapter we will suggest that curriculum development is an important area of professional development for all practitioners in education, but especially for teachers, who are responsible for the day-to-day management of the curriculum and for interpreting it in specific contexts with particular groups of children. It presents opportunities to work together with others and to constantly review day-to-day work.

Competence and professional development

The notion of 'competence' has become important in recent years and it is fundamental to professional practice and practice-based learning. Competence can be understood as 'what a person can do well' or 'what we can see' when a person carries out their work. In professional practice there can be no competence without knowledge and understanding, indeed, basic professional competence is usually considered to comprise knowledge, understanding, attitudes and skills. One of the roles of initial professional education courses is to ensure that their graduates have the basic, essential levels of knowledge and skill and that these newly qualified professionals understand how to develop these further. As expertise develops, a practitioner becomes increasingly flexible and confident in applying their experience to new situations, using internalised knowledge and intuitive thinking, yet being able to incorporate new information with their existing ideas. Schon (1983) used the term 'reflective practitioner' for expert practitioners who are able to use theories, developed over time, through practice, and to deal with unexpected occurrences. Competent professional practitioners therefore always reflect on their actions.

Curriculum as the heart of teaching

How then, are the ideas about professional development and professional competence applicable to curriculum planning and development? Curriculum development is the core of teachers' practice and is one of the specialist aspects of their work. The ability to work with a school curriculum is one of the ways in which teachers are distinguished from other professional practitioners. The management of curriculum thus contributes to teachers' professionalism.

Curriculum teaching and learning are interactive processes which involve complex links between characteristics of the pupils, features of the curriculum and the way it is presented. Through the processes of planning and reflecting on the curriculum in action, the skilled teacher will develop detailed awareness of each of these aspects. This is what underpins differentiation.

Curriculum development must also be based on *an analytical process*. Firstly,

21

in planning the curriculum there will be analysis of:

the children's strengths and needs;
the curriculum area;
the role of adults;
the resources to be used.

Then, in evaluating teaching and learning the teacher will integrate all of these elements and will analyse what happened.

As language is one of the main concerns of this book, the analysis at each of these points will involve language. The language strengths and needs of each child will be considered in the context of their overall learning needs; the language of the particular curriculum area will be examined and used as an important element of the teaching and learning; as adults are part of this process, their language will be an important 'tool' which may facilitate or obstruct the children's learning; resources, including those of the human variety, will be carefully selected or designed to support and enhance language. Figure 2.1 reminds us of the three important contributors to the language used in teaching and learning the curriculum, the language of the child, the adult(s) and of the curriculum itself.

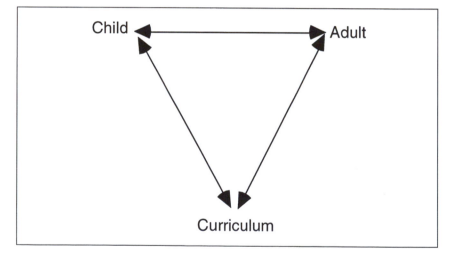

Figure 2.1 The interaction of language in curriculum development

Processes of curriculum development

The interactive and analytical processes of curriculum development will involve planning, carrying out the plan and finally, reviewing and evaluating what went on. For some practitioners this will be an explicit cycle, written down, using detailed plans and record sheets. Other practitioners may rely more on what is 'in their head', although with the recent heavier emphasis on school development and external scrutiny through inspection we should expect curriculum planning in most settings in the UK now to be transparent and available for others to see. Communication and collaboration between colleagues will be important contributors to the process if adults are to be seen as resources to support children's achievements.

In sketching the processes of curriculum development we have raised some important ideas which will recur throughout the chapters of this book. We have suggested that curriculum development is *cyclical*. It is recursive as the process goes back, reviewing what has happened and using this information to inform the next stage and it progresses, in stages, constantly moving on and being refined. *Interaction* is also an important notion. There will be interaction between the stages of development, each step being dependent on the one before and influencing the one which follows. Interaction between people will be critical if, firstly the adults are to work together and combine their creative ideas. Interaction is also an essential component of much teaching and learning in schools. There is interaction between children and adults and between pupils. Inevitably, much of this interaction takes place using language, either spoken or written. Individual and group-based curriculum activities also interact with a wider environment in that they are part of a whole-school system and indeed, of a national educational system. No parts can be considered completely autonomously in isolation. The third, important notion is *reflection*. The Concise Oxford Dictionary gives one definition of the verb *to reflect* as 'go back in thought' 'consult with oneself' and the noun *reflection* as 'reconsideration' 'mental faculty dealing with products of sensation and perception' 'idea arising in the mind, mental or verbal'. This intellectual, thoughtful activity will determine the quality and the appropriateness of the curriculum for pupils. It will also ensure that the engagement in curriculum development is stimulating and motivating for the adults involved.

Curriculum development as practitioner research

It may seem a large jump to associate curriculum development with research but the two have many features in common. We propose that the processes of developing appropriate teaching and learning activities for pupils can be recognised as a form of small-scale, practitioner research.

Lawrence Stenhouse, an important contributor to thinking and practice in curriculum development, defined research as 'sytematic inquiry made public' (Stenhouse 1975). The idea of curriculum development as 'systematic inquiry' has already been justified by suggesting that it involves careful, step-by-step planning and reflection. Whatever its scale, research depends on carefully chosen methods so that, if asked, 'how did you do that and why did you do it that way?' the researcher has a well thought out answer. This would certainly apply to the differentiation of curriculum activities which must always be well reasoned. It is perhaps less easy to see how curriculum development is 'made public'. However, making something public can be at many levels and we should not only think of media on a large scale such as books, journals and newspapers. Whilst we have, indeed, made public some specific examples of curriculum practice in this book, material can be made public within a particular environment, such as a school or service and it can be disseminated, not only through printed paper, but by verbal presentation and discussion at an interpersonal level. The processes described above, of collaboration and communication between colleagues, are forms of sharing and dissemination of ideas which can be important to the process of further thinking and development.

There is a particular form of research which is often recommended for practitioners who wish to improve their practice. It is known as *action research.* Action research shows many of the characteristics which we have noted to be typical of curriculum planning and development. It can provide a framework for the development of practice. One frequently-quoted definition of action research is as follows:

> A form of self-reflective inquiry undertaken by participants in social situations in order to improve the rationality and justice of their own practices, their understanding of those practices and the situations in which the practices are carried out. (Carr and Kemmis 1986, p. 162)

We can go through this description, linking it with what we have already asserted of curriculum development. 'Self-reflective inquiry' should, by now, need no further explanation. Thoughtful, reflective practitioners are vital if children with a range of abilities and needs are to have access to the curriculum. The idea of participants in social situations however, is perhaps considered more unusual in research. Research is often thought of as objective and experimental, perhaps taking place in laboratories or other 'non real' settings. This type of research may set out to test a theory or hypothesis or to check on some existing 'knowledge'. There are clearly questions about how laboratory research can provide us with insight into people in their environments and for this reason, different types of research are needed. Curriculum activities in the school system are frequently social activities and in these cases it is obvious that people are necessary. The children must be included and the adults are critical players in the success or failure of curriculum activities. The participants cannot be controlled in an experimental way and the research process must allow for unpredicted and unplanned-for reactions. The people are 'insiders' who play a critical part in the exploration and need to collaborate and communicate for the process to be successful. Returning again to the idea of reflection, in action research for

24

curriculum development, one of the purposes will be to think things through, understand better what is going on and, hopefully, use this knowledge to improve things further. Indeed, when considered like this, it becomes clear that 'knowledge' is flexible and constantly changing. The participants are developing their own ideas and knowledge because of what they observe and experience. Action research is often described as 'emancipatory'. The insights and under-standing gained can be liberating. In cyclical curriculum development, practitioners are enabled to take control of their decisions and actions and, although working within the boundaries of an education system or a prescribed curriculum, they use their own initiatives and professional knowledge creatively and purposefully.

Action research cycles

There is a cyclical process to action research and we will show how the cycles or spirals which are characteristic of action research can provide the framework on which to base curriculum planning and development.

Our daily working lives are filled with questions: What is the best way of helping this child? How can we make our curriculum policy work better? How can a classroom practitioner make more efficient use of the time allocated? Practitioners will have plenty more similar questions.

All research, on whatever scale, is based on questions and it is just as valid to research questions about the individual needs of a child or a school as it is to ask questions about new cures for cancer or how to reduce atmospheric pollution. The first stage in an action research project, as in curriculum planning, is to identify the area of concern and interest and to frame it as a question or questions which can be explored. Below are just a few ways in which curriculum development can start with a question:

'How can we help this child to gain something from science?'

'What could we do to provide meaningful experiences of modern foreign languages for this group of pupils?'

'How could the speech and language therapist and teacher collaborate effectively in planning the curriculum?'

More questions will become apparent in subsequent chapters of this book.

The cycles of action research go forward in a staged process of exploration, planning, action and review.

Stage 1: Exploration. The first stage of any effort to address such questions will be to examine carefully what is already happening. This is the first, essential step towards improving a situation or considering new ways of doing anything. Organisational development will often define this as the 'where are we now?' stage, which will be followed by 'where do we want to get to?' and 'how will we know when we are there?'. There are similar stages in all development work and although one person may initiate the stages, they should not be undertaken in isolation. If there are questions about the curriculum or about individual children or groups of children, other people will have ideas. This means discussing the question with colleagues and reading around it. It is important, before beginning any new venture, to discover whether anyone else has explored a similar question. How do other people understand and explain issues related to the question? For example, if the questions are about ways of developing support for children in a school, it would be important to read about, or to brainstorm, how people define 'support'; if the questions are about better implemention of the curriculum policy in a school, practitioners will want to look at some literature on policy development and how successful policy implementation has been described; perhaps similar policies from other schools could be examined.

This first stage of exploration can be an important influence on thinking and will raise the issues and ideas for the next stage, which is the formation of a plan of action.

The critical friend

At this point, it is appropriate to introduce the idea of the critical friend, a notion which is often referred to in reflective practice. The concept of reflective practice and action research as collaborative activities has already been raised. Practitioners who work successfully together communicate with each other and comment on each other's ideas and actions. The term 'critical friend' suggests that these people are trusted, yet able to question and challenge each other in a constructive way. They can act as a sounding board and a testing ground for ideas and when they do this, thinking can be extended and can develop further. The use of critical friends may require some practice if the members of a work group are not used to taking time together to discuss their plans and actions. However, with time, people can come to value the observations and reflections of colleagues and regard the experience as an investment of their time which has a pay-off in improved practice. Therefore, throughout the stages of action research and of curriculum development, communication and discussion with others are necessary.

Stage 2: Planning. The planning stage, is likely to be a paper exercise which takes account of the information gained at Stage 1. The plan on paper, or in another visible, readable form, is important so that there is something to which all participants can refer. The plan will state what is going to happen, where responsibilities will lie and what will be needed to carry out the plan effectively. Additionally, it will need to include clear information on how the action will be monitored so that participants will know how sucessful their plan was.

Stage 3: Action. In this stage the plan is carried out. Now, the plan on paper begins to interact with some rather unpredictable elements. These elements are usually people, in social settings. It is a fact that many schemes on paper become very different in practice. The responses of people can rarely be anticipated exactly and various aspects of the plan may work very differently in reality. The system for monitoring and recording the action will be important if the objectives of developing practice are to be realised.

Stage 4: Review. This stage is a review of what happened when the plan on paper was tried out in practice. The record of what happened is necessary and the presence of critical friends can be especially useful here. They will contribute their ideas on what worked well and what may have gone wrong. They may be able to suggest an alternative course of action for the next stage.

By now, the cyclical, staged nature of action research should be evident. In theory, it can go on for ever, in a constant process of doing and reviewing. However, in most cases reality prevails but, at the very least, an action research project must involve one complete cycle of planning, doing, reviewing and carrying out a further plan based on the experiences of the first action.

The curriculum planning cycle

The process of planning, reflecting, acting on a plan and then recording and evaluating the outcomes is an important aspect of day-to-day work. For the majority of practitioners, it is a cycle which constantly goes around in their heads. Many practitioners would not describe themselves as 'researchers' but this is exactly what they are doing when trying out ideas and then modifying them according to what happens in practice. It seems to convey exactly what is happening when curricular activities are planned and developed for children. The creation of suitable teaching and learning activities must be based on a staged process with a clear rationale and must always be open to change in the light of experience and new information.

In Chapters 3 to 10, all of the practitioners had a brief to undertake curriculum planning for their pupils who all had special educational needs with reference to their language development. Whereas language is commonly the vehicle for teaching and learning in the curriculum, these practitioners were challenged by children for whom this could not be assumed. Their needs in language development had to be met *at the same time* as their entitlement to the curriculum.

In identifying curriculum development as a cyclical, reflective process, it is possible to identify similar stages to those noted for action research. The stages are all based on the identification of a question or questions about how a particular aspect of the curriculum can be developed for a child or group of children in a particular setting.

Stage 1: Exploration. This stage will consist of reviewing and exploring issues relevant to a curriculum management plan. The components of the review will include the children, with particular reference to their language strengths and needs, the curriculum area and other factors specific to the context. Each of these will have relevance to the subsequent plan.

A knowledge of the pupils and their current levels of achievement is clearly necessary for any teaching. When different views of the child are available, from different members of a professional team, these will need to be combined. Parents too will contribute essential information on their child's background experiences and preferences. In the case of children with language and communication difficulties, teachers may work with speech and language therapists who will have made detailed assessments of a child's linguistic understanding and expressive abilities and the skills which underpin these. Teachers' evaluations of a child's communication skills in the interactions of a classroom, combined with a therapist's information on specific aspects of language, will be vital background for the curriculum plan.

Other colleagues too will contribute their specialist information. Learning support assistants (sometimes called special needs assistants, classroom assistants or a variety of other titles) may be appointed to support individual children who have special educational needs. They will build up important information from their experience of a child and how they may respond to particular circumstances. The assistants should be included in the group of practitioners who collaborate as critical friends.

Stage 1 continues with the exploration of the curriculum. Knowledge about the pupils will be combined with information about the requirements of the curriculum, clarified at different levels. For example, national guidelines will provide the broad framework within which schools will develop their curriculum policies. These, in turn, will be interpreted by classroom practitioners, for the needs of a range of children.

Subject areas are linked with particular use and meaning of language, which may be different from its meaning in other settings. For example, in maths, the word 'times' may be used for multiplication. In history, the same word may be used to denote 'times past'. This is different again from its use in the question 'How many times did Henry the Eighth marry?'. In this book, in Chapter 9 the teacher uses the words 'high' and 'low' to describe musical notes. These words can also be used to describe size, as, for example, in a 'high building' or a 'low seat'. If the language required to teach a particular aspect of the curriculum is analysed at this initial exploration stage, practitioners will be in a better position to undertake appropriate planning of the teaching and learning activities. They will become aware of how their own language will be used.

A third aspect for exploration at this stage relates to the particular context of the provision made for the pupil or group of pupils. This will include the number of adults available and their background and experience and the physical and material resources. The gathering and exploration of all of this information will enable the practitioners to assess 'where they are' and to consider 'where they would like to go', in terms of the children's learning and their teaching.

Stage 2: Planning. The process of curriculum planning must accommodate specific knowledge of pupils' language needs and the language of the curriculum together with keen awareness of the language used by adults. The planning stage therefore will involve the combining of familiar knowledge and skills with new information in every context. Plans also need to be transparent and explicit so that everyone involved is aware of the activities to be undertaken and the rationale for them. In the chapters which follow in this book, several of the practitioners discovered a need to clarify their plans and to prepare them in a form which was available to everyone.

Planning the curriculum is almost synonymous with planning for differentiation. As a wider range of children's needs are encountered in the classroom, their entitlement to the curriculum will be realised through the teaching and learning opportunities offered to them. The planning process will focus on two central aspects, what is taught and how it is taught.

Curriculum content, what is taught, will have been discussed in the explorations at Stage 1. It involves particular areas of knowledge and skills. Amongst the skills will be those relating to language and communication, which are cross-curricular skills, important for learning at every level. At the planning stage decisions will have to be made on the precise nature of these and how they will be promoted. Planning for how the curriculum will be taught will involve decisions about the style, strategies and organisation of teaching and decisions about whether aspects are taught discreetly from a subject basis or whether they are best addressed in a variety of cross-curricular ways. It is important to plan a number of ways of presenting and 'revisiting' learning so that pupils have the optimum opportunities to learn in their preferred way.

Differentiation through language is always important but it will have particular significance when pupils have specific linguistic difficulties. This form of differentiation may involve the teacher in explaining an activity to one pupil or to a group in a different way from the rest of the class in order to ensure success. It will certainly mean that different forms of expression will be expected from different children. Some for example, will speak their responses in full, clear utterances; others may sign their responses or may point to symbols prepared for them. Pupils may be asked to do completely different activities to show their understanding and knowledge of the same thing. One pupil may draw a series of pictures to retell a story or sequence of events whilst another will be asked to write a paragraph.

There are many other forms of differentiation to be considered at the planning stage. For example:

Differentiation by resources will mean that a variety of equipment is used and selected for the pupils so that they are enabled to complete an activity: for example, worksheets will be designed with different reading levels; large dice or pencil grips will be given to some children. Special equipment may be needed if pupils have physical disabilities, visual or hearing difficulties. It will be important that in the planning it is made clear who is responsible for such equipment and for checking that it is working effectively.

The teacher, or another adult, may focus more attention on some pupils than others. Planning will determine the levels of independent learning appropriate for different pupils and whether some will be given specific help and support.

Carefully planned organisation and grouping may be used so that, for example, pupils can work together and assist each other. Children with different linguistic abilities can be grouped to promote communication.

Differentiation by outcome will be an important aspect of planning and target setting which will focus on what is to be realistically expected of pupils as their personal best effort. Pupils can be expected to produce work of different quality or quantity from each other because the teacher knows what is 'good work' for them as individuals.

One of the aims of the planning stage will be to combine the ideas of a group of colleagues and to ensure that all are aware of the resulting plan. Whatever form this takes, some important factors should be evident.

- There should be a clear rationale for the planned activities. No one should be in doubt about why they are planned. Perhaps the most basic reason will be 'because national guidelines require it' but there should also be more specific reasons in which everyone can believe.
- Long- and short-term aims and objectives should be clear. Every lesson plan is linked with a broader plan, perhaps for half a term or a whole term. Within the plan there will be aims, not only for the group of pupils but for

individual children. The aims and objectives should be explicit. In particular, in addition to overall aims and objectives in curriculum areas, the plans will need to be clear in their identification of the language needs of the pupils. Wherever possible, pupils should be involved and made aware of intended outcomes.

- The plan will also show what will take place as differentiated work with the children. It will be necessary to identify the activities and how they are linked with the proposed learning outcomes for the pupils. It will be especially important that the plan indicates how the curriculum will be made accessible to the pupils. It will be clear how children will be supported by resources and how they will be grouped. The roles and responsibilities of adults will be explicit.

The final component of the plan document will state how the processes of the teaching and learning will be recorded so that there is evidence of what took place and what may need to be done next.

In many cases, it will be helpful to develop a pro forma for curriculum planning which will include:

The long-term aims.

The short-term aims and objectives for the particular session or sessions.

The content of the teaching and how this will make explicit the aims and objectives of the teaching.

The extent to which the pupils will be involved in, and/or made aware of the intended learning outcomes.

How the teaching will incorporate the overall spoken and written language needs of either the whole group of pupils or those of one or two individual pupils.

How resources (human and other) will be used to support the pupils in their learning.

How the curriculum will be differentiated to meet the needs of all pupils.

How outcomes will be recorded.

Reflection on the pro forma and discussion of the plan, by the group of colleagues involved, should help to objectively appraise the planning.

Stage 3: Action. Continuing to formulate curriculum development as action research means that Stage 3 can be identified as 'action'. In other words, it is the stage when teaching and learning (of pupils) take place. Planning exercises on paper may not be realised totally as intended. The interaction of people with what has been planned can never be predicted exactly and it is unlikely that everything will run smoothly. The action stage must always be considered as part of a continuous process of improvement and refinement. For this reason, the recording of what goes on in lessons is vital.

Reflection and objective observation can be difficult for people directly involved in teaching activities. The pace must be maintained and there can be little opportunity to do anything but focus completely on the pupils and their activities. There are a number of possibilities which practitioners can consider in order to record what goes on. The planning of the session may include designation of adults to act as observers at different points in the session. They may have a particular aspect of the session as their focus. For example, they may be asked to note the responses of a particular child or group or they may be asked to record the actions or the language of a particular adult. The planning may provide for recording, by video or on audiotape, of parts or all of the lesson. Alternatively, it should be possible to make notes or discuss the lesson as soon as possible after it has taken place so that it is fresh in the minds of the participants who planned it. A few moments in conversation with pupils at the conclusion of a lesson may also contribute to evidence on how it went.

Stage 4: Review. The record of the lesson, whether available on a videotape, as a verbal discussion between colleagues or in another form, provides the opportunity to review and reflect upon the experience of the lesson.

The review will consider the choice and balance of tasks and activities and how these met the curriculum aims. The involvement and support of adults and the interactions with pupils will be considered in terms of appropriateness of support and with particular reference to the language used. An important contributor to this aspect will be the use of resources, classroom organisation, mode of presentation of task(s) and the pupils' responses to these. All of these views will culminate to provide evidence of the pupils' learning. With regard to the original step-by-step description of the planning process and how it was realised in the classroom, it should be possible to identify what worked well and what aspects should now be changed.

Conclusion

The cyclical processes of managing the curriculum should be evident. Practitioners need to see themselves as problem solvers who amass considerable amounts of evidence every day. In order to sift through evidence and use it productively, a systematic and collaborative procedure can be helpful.

In the chapters which follow, there are examples of practitioners' efforts to plan and manage the curriculum for children described as having language and communication difficulties. The cycles which are presented do not end with perfection. They need to be seen as elements in a continuing process. The outcomes are found not only in achievements of pupils but in the development in knowledge and skills of the professionals who work together.

Chapter 3

Interaction in Science

Introduction

This chapter looks at learning through experiential tasks with peers and being able to talk about what has been learnt. The curriculum area involves a cross-curricular topic, which includes early Science, English and Design and Technology. Science is particularly appropriate because learning through experience and 'hands on' activity has been a recommended approach for some time. For example, in the 1960s, the Nuffield programme for science teaching emphasised an approach to learning through discovery. This approach has been endorsed more recently:

> hands on experience is a vital part of Primary science and children should be encouraged whenever possible to handle scientifically interesting objects and to make working models. (Womack 1988, p. 113)

The chapter discusses the planning and evaluation of a three-week cycle of teaching and learning and in particular two lessons, at the beginning and end of the cycle.

For young learners with language and communication difficulties the challenge is the interface between their cognitive learning and their ability to use language to describe and talk about what they have learnt. This chapter looks at how four infant school learners with a range of communication difficulties work together to learn and to develop communication skills to talk about electricity.

A further feature of this chapter concerns the collaboration and liaison between professionals. The chapter takes the support teacher's perspective and the liaison is between her, the class teacher and the speech and language therapist in developing the teaching/learning environment for this group of children. It also examines the criteria they developed for selecting the children for the learning group. Together they develop aims, learning activities and evaluation formats and processes.

Finally, this chapter looks at the issue of self-assessment by children of their own learning progress. It is an empowering mechanism for all learners yet is often not offered to young learners and rarely to learners with difficulties. The teachers' use of self-assessment becomes a valuable and powerful support to interactive learning as well as an insightful assessment mechanism.

First, let us begin by exploring the demands of the Key Stage 1 Science and the needs of the group of learners involved.

Curriculum areas

In the National Curriculum document (DfEE 1995a) at Key Stage 1 children are encouraged to develop and use a variety of communication skills and techniques involving speaking and listening, observation, investigation and response to information within their environment. The children were in Year 2, and aged between 6 and 7 years and studying at Key Stage 1, levels 1 and 2. The class teacher and support teacher with the involvement of the speech and language therapist were developing the cross-curriculum theme 'Toys'. It lent itself to developing aspects of the Science curriculum as well aspects of the curriculum in English and Design and Technology. The particular Attainment Target was concerned with electricity in the Science curriculum. Developing an electric circuit offered a wide range of learning opportunities and development of skills across all three areas of the curriculum.

The challenge that the children in this group presented was that in some contexts of learning they appeared to be able to learn and achieve through practical activities but they did not progress in developing curriculum vocabulary, communication skills and generalising knowledge to show concept development. For example, in a practical session, one child was investigating the different states of water, namely when water was frozen and boiled. After the activity, the child stated and pictorially recorded that 'ice is a solid and water is a liquid' which suggested that he had learnt about the different states of water from the activity. However, when he was asked, the child could not suggest or find other 'solids' in the room, which raises a query about his concept development. He seemed to have learnt the vocabulary and sentence structure appropriate for the activity but did not seem to have learnt the underlying concept. Thus, his learning was contextually and situationally restricted and his use of language may not have been supporting his learning. This child, and others with similar difficulties, needs to develop cognitive learning through experiential activities which are continually mediated by language. Thus, language is intimately linked with activity as one of the tools for learning.

An important concern was achieving a balance between twin priorities. That is, achieving individual targets as developed through the Individual Educational Programmes (IEPs) for each child with recognised statemented needs, and the curriculum learning targets as described in the National Curriculum. In group discussion between the three professionals involved, the priority was identified as developing individual skills within the context of the topic. The ability to listen, contribute, share and take 'risks' in practical activities was fundamental in practical, discovery-based learning. For the children in this group 'curiosity and a questioning attitude need to be fostered and encouraged' (Womack 1988, p. 115).

The children

The children in the group were being integrated from a language unit placement into a mainstream infant class. Initially, an established class group of six children was selected but on the advice of the support teacher and the speech and language therapist a group of four was thought to be a more manageable size of group for interacting, observing and recording. The children were also selected according to a set of criteria based on classroom observations (15 categories), teachers assessments and the children's IEPs. On the basis of mutual and complementary strengths and difficulties the children were selected. Three of the children chosen were being integrated from the language unit and the fourth child had always been in the mainstream class and was chosen because his educational progress was causing concern.

The following are brief sketches of the children and their language skills given by the support teacher. The names used are not their real names.

Dorothy is seven years old and has a specific language difficulty. Her auditory processing skills are slow and there are gaps in her conceptual development. She has been taught in a small language group for two years and is now fully integrated within the host school. Whilst she can complete structured and familiar tasks, observations by the support teacher indicate that her pragmatic difficulties are hindering her application of acquired skills and ability to relate appropriately to other children and experiences. She rarely contributes in class except to inform the teacher that someone is misbehaving and has few strategies to attempt unfamiliar tasks or situations. Her Individual Education Plan and her Therapy Care Plan highlight the need to focus on her pragmatic difficulties, such as awareness of other children, as well as connecting ideas and reinforcing skills learned in the classroom to everyday applications.

Eve is six years old and has been integrated following one year in the language centre. She has severe expressive language delay with associated difficulties relating to self-confidence, independence and social communication. In class she is extremely slow in both verbal and written responses and rarely completes tasks without individual support. The group would focus on developing skills to encourage her to demonstrate her conceptual understanding and to encourage more confident responses and self-confidence.

Colin is also six years old and has expressive language difficulties. He has a poor speech sound system and his verbal and written sentence structure is very muddled, sometimes resulting in frustration and inappropriate behaviour. Colin is also now fully integrated within the host school with support. He and Dorothy have inevitably been educated closely together and it has been observed that the relationship has become competitive and often comments between the two children are detrimental to self-esteem and attention. This was a factor in the selection of the group but the inclusion of the fourth child was carefully selected to facilitate Colin becoming less dependent on the children from the language centre. Additionally, the group would focus on the Individual Education Plan and Care Plan which, for Colin, have the aim to slow his speech rate and structure sentences more accurately by hearing accurate modelling within a confident atmosphere and to work collaboratively with a mainstream child.

The fourth member of the group, Kit, was carefully selected to complement the children from the language centre. Kit is a quiet child who has a medical condition that results in poor fine motor control. He also speaks and writes very slowly and tentatively. Whilst his conceptual understanding and use of vocabulary appears age-appropriate, he rarely completes tasks without support and his inability to sit still and take turns is of increasing concern to his class teacher and parents. Kit does not have a Statement of Special Educational Need but his class teacher has targeted a need to develop attention skills and self-motivation. The group would also allow a closer observation of his skills within a less distracting environment.

The children from the language centre are familiar with the setting of group rules and individual targets during language group sessions and it was agreed that Kit would benefit from this practice as he would have to take responsibility for his own behaviour in one specific area.

Planning

In this section, issues such as planning the sessions as well as identifying the curriculum and individual targets are discussed, together with discussion about the location of the sessions.

Venue

Since the whole Year 2 class was involved in learning about the cross-curricular theme, 'Toys', as well as about the specific topic of the electric circuit, a classroom display was mounted of relevant electrical resources. However, all the teaching/learning sessions with the small group were segregated from the main class activities. The first session with the group of four learners was in the classroom on the 'carpet area' adjacent to the display to maximise the inclusion of the materials in the display in the first session's teaching/learning activities. In the sessions which followed over the next three weeks, the group were withdrawn to a quieter area immediately outside the classroom. The language centre was suggested as a teaching venue because video recording of the group would have been possible. Against this was the chance that Dorothy, Colin and Eve might have been distracted by being in the presence of their previous teacher and friends.

The one hour sessions in the three-week cycle were led by the support teacher although carefully planned in collaboration and liaison with the class teacher and therapist. Two sets of aims were developed: curriculum attainment targets and also individual learning targets. The activities and materials were planned and extensive evaluation formats and processes were developed. The first session was planned, recorded and evaluated in detail to facilitate substantial reflection and revision which, in turn influenced the planning and evaluation of the final teaching/learning session three weeks later.

Curriculum aims

The curriculum aims were drawn up using the National Curriculum Orders for Science (Key Stage 1, Attainiment Target 4), English (Key Stage 1, Attainment Target 1) and Design and Technology (Key Stage 1, Attainment Targets 1 and 2). Other sources were also used, namely *Folens Science in Action* (Harrison *et al.* 1992) and *Essentials for Science: Electricity and Magnetism* (Mackay 1996). A draft list of learning outcomes was drawn up, and from them group and individual outcomes were identified as well as areas for differentiation.

SCIENCE

Taken from *Folens Science in Action* (Harrison *et al.* 1992)

AT1 Scientific Investigation

Encourage children to use and develop their scientific knowledge and understanding.
Involve children and their teachers in promoting ideas and seeking solutions.
Promote at first hand the exploration of materials and events.
Encourage the appreciation of the need for safe and careful action.
Encourage children to question what they did and suggest improvements.

AT4 Physical Processes

Children should be made aware of some of the uses of electricity in the

classroom and in the home, and the dangers of misuse.
They should experience simple activities using bulbs, buzzers, batteries and wires, and investigate materials to discover those which conduct electricity and those which do not.

Taken from *Essentials for Science: Electricity and magnetism* (Mackay 1996)

Provide experience in observing, predicting, recording, measuring and making hypotheses.
Provide opportunities for children to share their ideas with others.
Develop an understanding of electricity words.
Make a bulb light up.
Make an electric circuit.
Provide opportunities to predict outcomes and test ideas.

Taken from *School Curriculum Plan for Year Two Topic; Toys*

- Describe the differences and similarities between materials.
- Be able to construct a circuit.
- Understand that a circuit with a break in it will not work.

ENGLISH

ATI Speaking and Listening

Level 1:   Talk about matters of immediate interest.
Listen to others and usually respond appropriately.
Convey simple meanings to a range of listeners, speaking audibly.

Level 2:   Show confidence in talking and listening, particularly where the topics interest them.
Show awareness of the needs of the listener by including relevant detail.
Speak clearly and use a growing vocabulary.
Listen carefully and respond with increasing appropriateness to what others say.

DESIGN AND TECHNOLOGY

AT1 Designing

Level 1 :   Generate ideas through shaping, assembling and rearranging materials and components.
Use pictures and words to convey what they want to do.

Level 2:   Reflect on ideas and suggest improvements.

AT2 Making

Level 1: Explain what they are making and which materials they are using.

Level 2: Select from a narrow range of materials and tools . . . and explain their choices.

Make judgements about the outcomes of their work.

The support teacher and the class teacher agreed on the following aims and learning outcomes for the three-week teaching/learning cycle.

The curriculum aims over the three weeks were:

- to construct an electric circuit
- to value and gain information from practical activities
- to develop skills of self-evaluation.

General learning aims were:

- to understand an electric circuit
- to handle equipment and
- to talk about it within a small group
- to share their ideas about the topic with others
- to develop their own ideas by listening and responding to others
- to know some topic-specific Science curriculum vocabulary.

Specific aims were:

- design and construct a simple electric circuit to light up a bulb on a cut-out Christmas tree
- understand and use topic-specific curriculum vocabulary
- work cooperatively with a partner
- maintain interest and attention during practical activity
- evaluate own achievement.

Individual aims

The individual aims were:

Dorothy: Listen and respond to other children's comments.

Colin: Take turns and not interrupt unnecessarily.

Eve: Respond quickly to questions or when it is her turn, without adult reassurance.

Kit: Sit still without sucking his fingers.

Differentiation

The individual targets for each child were developed and differentiated further. For example, Dorothy was to be encouraged to ask her partner for comments with modelling by the teacher and peers. Colin was to be reminded by 'gentle hands on knees' to wait his turn and then receive praise when he did. Eve was to have help with fine motor tasks, such as handling the crocodile clips. Kit was to be given opportunites to move places and be 'mobile'.

Communication

The support teacher used spoken language throughout the sessions and also some signs. Liaising with the therapist, Dorothy, Colin and Eve, but not Kit, knew some signs from the Paget Gorman system. Apart from not wishing to exclude Kit, using Paget Gorman signs was not appropriate for the specific curriculum vocabulary related to the topic on electric circuits. The preferred way of communicating was using spoken language to mediate a multi-sensory approach to handling and using the materials in the activities and for peer interaction.

Collaboration

From the above it is clear that there was much collaboration and liaison between the support teacher and therapist as well as the class teacher. The support teacher also included the teacher in the language centre in consulting about working with the selected group of children. Further examples are shown when she discussed with the therapist the vocabulary and concepts needed and ways in which they could be introduced in the sessions, as well as in planning the evaluation. The support teacher also liaised with the teacher in the language centre about ways in which the children's 'interest' and 'understanding' could be effectively evaluated. She also discussed with the class teacher and therapist ways of recording the achievements of the children in such a way that they could use the information in planning individual programmes.

Planning the session

There were nine planned activities in the first hour-long session.

1. Members of the group to introduce themselves.
   Rules of the group explained by the teacher.
   Individual targets explained by the teacher.

2. Teacher to explain that the group is going to 'investigate' the display materials (write up and explain this word).

3. Each child to ask another to select a particular item.

4. Allocate pairs and allow time for each pair to handle and talk about items.

5. Each member to report back to the whole group.

6. As a group, to name the items on display, match each with the written label and practise the vocabulary.

7. Children's choice of game: Kim's game or Feely bag game; encourage group cooperation in choosing.

8. Teacher to remind each child of individual target; each child to self-evaluate, followed by group comment. Show group recording form.

9. Each child to say what they have learnt to the group.

The teacher felt that the session was too structured and introduced some flexibility. Investigation of the equipment was done at an early stage, partners were swapped, and a Feely bag game was available if needed.

The learning outcomes of the session were:

- to name the electrical items, e.g. wires, battery, bulb
- to be able to describe in some detail one of the electrical resources
- to be aware of their individual targets
- to say one thing that they have learnt during the session.

Planning evaluation

There are two stages to the evaluation. First, there is record-keeping which collects the data about the children's performance. Second, there is an evaluation of the quality of learning which has taken place among group members.

Discussion between the teachers and therapist about the most effective and feasible method of record keeping focused on the issues of recording and evaluating the children's practical activity, and recording and evaluating the children's understanding, bearing in mind that they did not always respond reliably to questions. With children who have language and communication difficulties, lack of teacher time and record-keeping skills often leads to inaccuracies and inadequacies in assessment and evaluation of learning.

There were four areas where information about the children's learning performance was needed and different ways of recording progress were used.

(a) *Curriculum targets* were recorded by the teacher in long hand, noting group and individual performance, after the session.

(b) *Specific social/learning behaviours,* such as fidgeting, interrupting, listening, initiating, predicting, were recorded on a 'tick' sheet format that was completed during the session and photocopied and given to appropriate colleagues.

(c) *Practical activities* were recorded in the topic book as evidence of the learning situation. The format design outlined the purpose and key aspects of the activity and was similar to the format for significant achievements used by the mainstream infant school.

(d) *Individual targets* were evaluated at the end of the session by each child and also by the whole group. This recording activity, which was suggested by the therapist, can increase children's awareness of their responsibility for their own learning and behaviour, as individuals and as a group. The information was recorded on a grid sheet format and kept by the teacher.

The teacher had outstanding queries about individual children. She was concerned about accurately recording the sentence structure in the responses of Colin and Eve. Other formats such as video recording and audio recording were not feasible, consequently the therapist recommended that the teacher note her own correct modelling of sentence structures and the content of talk during the free play session. If this method did not provide satisfactory record data then the therapist as an observer would take notes. Finally, to manage Dorothy's difficulty of being slow to respond and possibly repeating other children's comments, she would be given the role of 'teacher' to sum up the activity to the group and perhaps later to the class.

Evaluation

The learning outcomes of the group were evaluated as well as the children's self evaluation of their learning.

In addition, the structure of the session and methods of record-keeping were evaluated.

Structure of session

The opening activities, introductions, explanations of rules and individual targets, were valuable because they established the responsibilities of the children and the children attended well. However, they took up a substantial amount of time and alone could have constituted the first session. Planning with future groups would need to take this into account.

The activities which focused on handling and talking about the equipment yielded low learning outcomes. The children had showed little interest in the display in previous weeks and it was clear that they needed adult guidance to interact with the display. This reflects the low latent curiosity with learners like the children in the group, cited by Womack earlier. The implication for future planning is to develop activities with the equipment which are more transparently goal orientated.

The structure of the session facilitated all the children naming the equipment and practising using the vocabulary. Only Kit spontaneously named the battery. All four children confused the use of 'electric' and 'electricity'. Future planning needs to introduce new curriculum-specific vocabulary in such a way as to check levels of knowledge (e.g. recognition, matching, spontaneous use) and to emphasise supported, staged introduction and familiarisation of new vocabulary at the appropriate level. The learning outcomes could reflect these stages.

The children's self and group evaluation came at the end of the session. It was largely a successful activity in terms of the learning outcomes:

- to be aware of their individual targets
- to say one thing that they have learnt during the session.

Two of the children, Dorothy and Kit, felt they had achieved, while the two others did not; Eve was silent and Colin cried and thought he had failed. As a group, Kit, Eve and Colin *passed* everyone, although Dorothy found fault with the others. The implications for future planning is to include these learning outcomes and to build on them, developing them to include notions of group support and awareness about levels and types of achievement.

The structured element of the session targeted aspects of curriculum language development but it did not facilitate interaction and cooperative learning. Few utterances were made by the children, either directed to the teacher or to each other. Kit made undirected comments, the girls said nothing and Colin remained morose when he could not have all the equipment. To improve interaction the teacher stopped record keeping of the children's behaviour and guided the activity by modelling questions and encouraging all the children to contribute. In her interaction with the teacher, Dorothy showed that she understood the significance of the wires connecting and electricity passing through metals but did not understand that the battery was the source of power. The teacher's interaction was needed to demonstrate Dorothy's level of achievement. The implications for future sessions is to plan activities which develop pragmatic aspects of the children's language. In addition, it would be important to have record-keeping methods of the children's language which do not exclude the teacher, who is a valuable facilitator.

Amendments to future sessions

Collating the implications from the evaluation, some clear directions emerge for amending future sessions. For example, the activities became more goal-orientated and focused on designing and constructing a working model of a Christmas tree that had a working bulb light. Cooperation and interaction would be focused on work in pairs rather than working in a group of four; Dorothy and Eve, Colin and Kit. The role of the teacher as language facilitator and assessor would be maintained, although her activity was amended. An initial activity where the resources would be 'bought' from the teacher facilitated labelling and description of the equipment. During the remainder of the session the teacher would facilitate and observe peer cooperation, communication and sharing of knowledge. The amended arrangement made feasible the record-keeping of performance and language use by the teacher. Video recording was not possible because the assistant was ill. The successful aspects of the opening activities would be maintained. Recapping the individual targets and rules would be brief because they were known to the children, and minor changes would be easy to introduce, such as the individual targets for Dorothy and Colin which would encourage cooperative talking.

43

The learning outcomes for the final session were amended and developed:

- construct a cut-out Christmas tree with a working light bulb on it
- select and name the electrical resources
- work with another child
- report their activities to the main class.

Final session

There were six planned activities for the final session:

1. Recapping individual targets.
2. Sharing individual designs; reminder of partner and task.
3. Children to decide what resources they need and in turn request them from the teacher using correct vocabulary.
4. Children in pairs to construct Christmas tree designs, while teacher observes and records.
5. Children to show tree to group and comments and suggestions made with support from teacher.
6. Models to be shown to class with explanations.

The overall outcome of the session was positive and the learning outcomes were achieved to varying degrees. All the children were excited and enthusiastic about the activities in the session, suggesting that a more goal-orientated approach is likely to be more motivating for this group of learners. They were all able to request by name the electric equipment they needed, although Dorothy named the crocodile clips as 'teeth'. Both groups constructed a cut-out Christmas tree with a working light bulb on it.

Working together in pairs showed individual communication skills and difficulties. For example, Dorothy's interaction difficulties showed by dominating Eve, although she asked for the tree she preferred to take it, and she could not answer questions from Eve but repeated the question form. Despite this there were indications of increased tolerance in her interactions with Eve. Eve on the other hand was submissive although she contributed appropriate ideas. Colin was reluctant to work with Kit's design but then he and Kit worked well together, taking turns, sharing and cooperating.

Both teachers were pleased with the outcome of the children's report of their activities to the main class. They decided to work this form of assessment into more areas of the curriculum. The children's strengths, weaknesses and learning progress were clearly demonstrated. For example, Eve, for the first time, showed self-esteem and confidence by speaking to the whole class and naming the equipment although she needed support and encouragement. Dorothy's pragmatic difficulties were evident in her interactions and also her difficulties understanding peer questions. Colin explained the sequence of making the tree using the vocabulary correctly and included Kit in his explanations. Although he repeated himself, what he said was relevant and concise. Kit's difficulties interacting with a larger group were clear, and he interrupted and sought attention, yet did not speak sufficiently loudly to the class when it was his turn. Both teachers noted that working in a small group prepared the four children for interacting with the larger group. It gave them and the teacher the opportunity to focus on the learning task, practice curricular language, develop interaction skills, as well as rehearse explanations and presentation skills.

Conclusion

This chapter has looked at how a small group of learners with communication difficulties have learnt interactively through experimental tasks with peers and been able to talk about what they have learnt. The important features of this study concern the aspects of curriculum chosen, the interactive learning, the planning and assessment and the collaboration of the professionals involved.

The curriculum area chosen was a cross-curricular topic, which included early Science, English and Design and Technology. Although cross-curricular topic work is not a feature of the national curriculum, it offers learners and teachers the opportunity to develop learning in more meaningful contexts. One of the findings from this study is that children with communication difficulties are more likely to interact with more practical and goal-orientated activities.

This small action research study is based around the planning and evaluation of a three week cycle of teaching and learning, in particular two lessons, at the beginning and end of the cycle. The design allows the professionals involved to identify and focus on short term learning outcomes which in turn form part of longer term aims. The study promoted consideration of more accurate and feasible record-keeping procedures which facilitated evaluation and further planning. The evaluations allowed the professionals to differentiate the children's learning needs from their communication needs and to plan future learning outcomes on this basis.

There are three main findings from this study.

- This group of learners with diverse communication needs progressed in their interaction and social skills when they were offered particular learning contexts. For example: having the opportunity to work in a small group and then in pairs, separated from the main class, where they could develop interactional and communicative skills; to learn and practice specific curriculum language; and to rehearse talking about what they had learnt.

Future study would need to explore more effective integration of the group into the main class.

- An influential finding for the professionals involved in the study was the power of self-assessment by the children of their own learning progress. The group of young learners with difficulties demonstrated individually and as a group that they were able to identify with, work towards and evaluate their learning targets. A progression of this empowering approach would be to encourage the children to identify their own communication needs and improvement targets.

- Finally, this study shows effective collaboration and liaison between two teachers and a therapist. The support teacher is the protagonist in the study and it is her initiatives which facilitate the liaisons with the class teacher, the speech and language therapist and the teacher in the language centre in order to develop the teaching/learning environment for this group of children. As such, it is a good model for other groups of professionals who may not work closely enough to feel that they constitute a 'team' yet who need to liaise, possibly through one co-ordinator, in order to explore innovative ways of teaching and supporting learning with pupils who have substantial interactional and communication difficulties.

Chapter 4

Teaching Science and English

Introduction

This chapter describes a cycle of teaching and evaluation in a language unit where the class teacher and learning support assistant work through curricular aims for Science and English as well as non-curricular aims for cooperative learning. There are eight children in the unit, who are boys and girls with mainly semantic and pragmatic difficulties. Two teaching and evaluation sessions are presented, which took place on two afternoons for one and a half hours over three weeks in the middle of the autumn term. The second session was planned and taught on the basis of the modifications following the evaluations of the first session.

The children

The children were between 7 and 10 years of age, that is Years 3 and 6 in junior school and working towards Key Stage 2 of the National Curriculum in England and Wales. Figure 4.1 provides information about the pupils' language and learning difficulties. The names are not their own.

Despite the children's differences in age and learning abilities their language needs were mainly in the areas of semantics and pragmatics. They were all intelligible although there were occasions when speech was mumbled. They could form short sentences and some were able to join sentences using conjunctions, such as 'and', 'then', ''cos'. However, they all had difficulty telling a sequence of events. They hesitated, showed difficulties referring back using correct pronouns, and had difficulties with organising a sequence of events. Semantic difficulties showed through use of 'empty' lexical items with no specific meaning, such as 'doing it', 'sort of', inaccurate use of words and word-finding difficulties. The corollary of semantic and pragmatic difficulties is problems in understanding what is said. The practitioner has to be aware of the need to present learning material in non-linguistic forms, and then in different linguistic forms at different language development levels. Regularly checking pupils' comprehension allows practitioners to pinpoint when and where pupils are having difficulties understanding.

Pupils' information

Child	Age	Difficulties
Peter	10	Semantic/pragmatic
Michael	10	Receptive/semantic/pragmatic
Angela	9	Semantic/word endings and function words
Jane	7	Pragmatic
Timothy	7	Semantic/pragmatic
Simon	7	Semantic/pragmatic
Raymond	7	Pragmatic
Roger	9	Receptive/semantic/pragmatic and difficulties in cooperative learning

Figure 4.1

The long-term aims and lesson objectives

The long-term aims in Science, English and the non-curricular area remained the same over the three-week period, yet within each lesson the learning objectives changed. Figures 4.2, 4.3 and 4.4 set out the aims and objectives for the first lesson.

Science curriculum: Physical properties

Aim		Learning objective
A	Investigate force	Gain an understanding of friction
B	Make careful observations and measurements	Carry out an experiment to investigate friction
C	Develop an understanding of a fair test	Say whether the test was fair/unfair
D	Use results to draw conclusions	Accurately measure distance car travelled in metres and centimetres. Say why the car travelled further on one surface rather than another
E	Record information in an appropriate manner	To record results as they do the experiment

Figure 4.2

English curriculum

Aim		*Learning objective*
A	Report factual information sequentially to the teacher and to the class	Present findings to the group verbally and explain what they did and why
B	To listen to factual evidence presented by others and discuss appropriately	To listen to each group present their findings
C	To listen to and follow instructions sequentially	To carry out verbal and written instructions accurately
D	Understand and use appropriate scientific vocabulary	Check understanding and use of following vocabulary: *slippery most slippery least slippery smooth rough ramp surface slope*

Figure 4.3

Non-curricular aim

Aim		*Learning objective*
A	To work cooperatively	Work with partner on car experiment Demonstrate confidence throughout task Discuss with partner rather than call on teacher for help when there is a problem

Figure 4.4

Individual lesson aims

Differentiation is an important aspect of working with a range of abilities and across age groups. Each had individual differentiated lesson aims. In Science every pupil followed the six learning objectives, except Jane who aimed for A to D, and Timothy who aimed for A only – 'Gain an understanding of friction'. In English (Fig 4.6) all the pupils followed the learning objectives except Timothy who aimed for the second objective only – 'To listen to each group present their findings'. All the pupils aimed to achieve the non-curricular object ive (Fig 4.7). Each pupil had certain objectives differentiated to meet their n

---

Science curriculum: Physical properties

Learning objective	*Differentiation*
A Gain an understanding of friction	(No individual differentiation)
B Carry out an experiment to investigate friction	Roger, Jane and Simon to have adult help
C Say whether the test was fair/unfair	Roger, Jane, Simon and Angela to recognise one variable and Peter, Michael and Raymond, two variables
D (i) Accurately measure distance car travelled in metres and centimetres	(No individual differentiation)
(ii) say why the car travelled further on one surface rather than another	Peter, Michael and Raymond to use the word 'friction'
E To record results as they do the experiment	(No individual differentiation)

Figure 4.5

English curriculum

Learning objective	*Differentiation*
A Present findings to the group verbally and explain what they did and why	Peter: without anxious breathing Michael: clear, slow articulation Raymond and Jane: concise Roger: sequence Angela: word endings Simon: past tense
B To listen to each group present their findings	Timothy: clear articulation Roger: look at speaker Jane: listen without interrupting
C Carry out verbal and written instructions accurately	Peter: adult help for written ones Roger and Jane: in correct sequence
D Check understanding and use of the following vocabulary: *slippery most slippery least slippery* *smooth rough* *ramp surface slope*	Peter: explain four target words Angela, Jane, Simon: explain six target words Raymond: explain eight target words

Figure 4.6

Non-curricular aim

Learning objective	*Differentiation*
A 1. Work with partner on car experiment	Roger: for 10 minutes Jane: without dominating Timothy: speaking
2. Demonstrate confidence throughout task	
3. Discuss with partner rather than call on teacher for help when there is a problem	

Figure 4.7

The first lesson

The aim of the lesson was to learn about friction and there were three main activities: watching the Science Challenge video about 'Slipping and Sliding', and two experiments. The teacher introduced the video and told the pupils what it would be about. After the video, the teacher discussed with the children what they thought *friction* was and asked for examples of the need to *increase friction* and the need to *reduce friction*.

The video was followed by the first experiment, called 'The tray test' which was planned to last about twenty minutes. The children gathered around one table while the teacher explained the tray test. The children were asked to collect four similar sized objects with flat bases. Each child named the four objects and the teacher wrote the words on the board. The children predicted which object would slide down the tray first. They each did the experiment on their own in their own space. Then they returned to the table and each child in turn demonstrated the experiment with the other children predicting the outcome and recorded their results on the sheet.

The second experiment was about friction affecting the distance a toy car could travel on different surfaces, and was planned to take about 50 minutes. The teacher checked that the children understood the key vocabulary: *ramp, slope, surface*, and explained to them what they were to do. In pairs, the children were to think of four different surfaces which the teacher wrote on the board. The children then chose a partner with whom they carried out the experiment and recorded their results on a sheet as they went along. The teacher and assistant circulated around each pair. To conclude, each group showed the others how they had done the experiment and what they had found out.

Pupil assessment

There were several forms of assessment built into the session, such as observation, discussion throughout the lesson and a tape recording of each child's explanation of the car experiment. In addition, the following day the children were asked questions about the session, which evaluated their knowledge in a cognitively demanding way with no contextual support. In addition, at the end of term, the Individual Educational Programmes were completed and curriculum notes written on each child's individual record.

The first session was evaluated for long-term aims and the lesson objectives. The lesson gave the children access to all the Science, English and non-curricular long-term aims.

Science

Aim A: Gain an understanding of friction
When asked about the tray experiment the following day, six children gave a good explanation of why object A came down faster than object B. Five of these children used the word 'friction'. However, Roger and Angela showed that they had not understood the experiment. Roger said that the tray was sticky while Angela said that gravity was pushing the rubber on, possibly confusing it with the lesson on gravity the previous week.

When asked to explain the word 'friction', five children were able to give a reasonable definition. The video was successful in introducing the concept and showed lots of examples of increasing and decreasing friction. The children were able to remember many examples but only Michael, Raymond and Jane did not confuse 'increased friction' and 'decreased friction', which are minimal opposites. Timothy was able to explain friction in the context of the tray experiment, but not out of context.

Aim B: Carry out an experiment to investigate friction
The lesson gave all the pupils the opportunity to investigate friction.

Aim C: Say whether the test was fair/unfair
The group comprehended the difference between a fair/unfair test in the context of the car experiment, but, except for two, they were unable to demonstrate it or understand it out of context. For example, only Simon and Peter appeared to have a concept of a fair test by using a ramp of consistent height, about two cubes high. The other pupils varied the ramp height at different times, often using the nearest object to prop up the card, regardless of the angle.

When an example of unfair testing was demonstrated by the teacher pushing one car but letting the other roll on its own, the pupils put up their hand to say it was not a fair test. However, when the children were telling the others about their experiment, none of them showed understanding of a fair test. Two examples from the children's transcripts illustrate this:

Example 1
Teacher: How did you make the test fair?
Angela: I put the metre at the back and then I check which centimetre it went to.

Example 2
Teacher: How did you make your test fair?
Roger: I put um these bricks under the card.

Aim D: Accurately measure distance car travelled in metres and centimetres
The pupils still had difficulties measuring, and using the words 'metres' and 'centimetres' appropriately. For the previous five weeks, as part of a maths topic, the group had been measuring in metres and centimetres. They made a 'metre mouse' (a small measuring instrument) but had only spent one lesson measuring in centimetres accurately. More practice was needed since two groups had the metre mouse the wrong way round at one point. The teacher noted that a revision lesson that morning might have been beneficial to the children so that the arithmetic task of measuring did not detract from the scientific focus.

The pupils showed different levels of understanding the task. For example, Raymond used a ruler instead of his metre mouse which led to inaccurate results. Roger did not start the measure at 0 centimetres, and confused the units of measurement, saying the distance was 61 metres instead of 61 centimetres. In contrast, Angela had the mouse in the right place but misread the number, 13 centimetres for 30 centimetres. The teacher noted that an adult attached to the two groups, at this point in the experiment, could have interacted with the learners with specific guidance.

Aim E: Say why the car travelled further on one surface rather than another
This question sought an application of the learners' knowledge. The teacher felt that two children would not be able to access this question. Of the six children asked, four gave good reasons, such as:

Angela: Because it's smooth and it went smoothly.
Peter: It was like soft and flat [pause] and hard.

However, Roger and Jane seemed to have no understanding of cause–effect:

Roger: 'Cos it was straight.
Jane: It was smoother than the floor 'cos there's lots of tables.

Aim F: Record results as they do the experiment
Three important evaluations and recommendations came from these results regarding recording results, reading and the worksheet. All children recorded the results of their car experiment as they went along but only two of the eight children recorded the results in the correct place. A maths lesson to revise this would have helped. A number of the children could not read the surface word and had to keep asking an adult. A picture with the written word would have helped. Following the tray experiment, only Raymond and Angela were confident about completing the worksheet on their own. The other children needed adult help. Thus, the format of the worksheet needed to be reconsidered.

English

Aim A: Present findings to the group verbally and explain what they did and why
The pupils found this task extremely difficult and only Angela came close to succeeding in it. The children were asked both to demonstrate to the group, and, at the same time, explain, what they had done. The presentation of each child was tape recorded and transcribed. Most of the pupils simply showed their findings to the class without speaking and had to be prompted by the teacher to give verbal explanations. Angela achieved the aim as well as her individual target, and two other children achieved their individual target but not the aim. The results were below expectations and the task was much less successful than planned for.

The teacher shared the transcripts with the speech and language therapist to plan together individual targets. The instruction, 'Tell the group how you did the experiment' was too demanding for most of the pupils' abilities, not so much in understanding the instruction, but more in the organisation which the response required. That is, not only did they have to demonstrate the sequence of events which they had followed, but at the same time they had to verbalise what they had done using language which supported the sequence, such as conjunction words, tense and modality markers and temporal adverbs. Angela demonstrated all these features:

> 'well I was [pause] well first I put the mouse on the floor straight then I put the car on the top and it went and I checked where where it had gone/it had went on 13 centimetres'

Children with language and communication difficulties like those in this group have difficulty organising and sequencing their actions. Their language usually reflects these organisational difficulties. The evaluation showed that pupils needed a range of self-reporting tasks to match their skills, such as demonstrating the sequence of events, presenting a visual display, giving a verbal description and explanation.

Aim B: To listen to each group present their findings
This aim is linked to the previous one, and seven of the eight pupils appeared attentive. Roger's interest in his peers' findings had not been established, and he was not attending while the other children were explaining. The teacher noted that it was a long period for the children to be attentive (about 15 minutes) and it might be more interesting for the pupils to have some children reporting each lesson rather than attempting to assess the whole class in detail.

Aim C: To carry out verbal and written instructions accurately
The instructions for the tray experiment were explicit, that is: 'Go and get four objects and then come and sit down', and the pupils showed no difficulties

Defining key vocabulary								
	Peter	Raymond	Roger	Angela	Timothy	Simon	Jane	Michael
slippery	√	√	√	√	√	√	√	√
most slippery	x	√	x	x	x	√	√	x
least slippery	x	√	x	x	x	√	√	x
smooth	√	√	√	√	√	√	√	√
rough	√	√	√	√	√	√	√	√
ramp	√	√	x	√	√	√	√	√
surface	√	x	x	x	x	√	√	√
slope	√	√	x	x	√	√	√	√

Figure 4.8

following them. However, they had more difficulties with instructions about the car experiment. This was most probably because they had to remember more than one instruction, and no visual clues or written checklist were given. Other difficulties showed when the children had found partners. Only Simon and Peter collected one set of equipment for their pair as requested. In the three other groups, each child collected a set of equipment and worked independently rather than with their partner.

While the children's lack of success on this aim could have been due to their limited understanding of verbal instructions, it could also have been because they could not yet work collaboratively.

Aim D: Check understanding and use of vocabulary
The video helped to establish three of the eight target words (*slippery, smooth, rough*). The visual impact of, for example, seeing a car on a slippery road, helped reinforce the new vocabulary. All eight children were able to give a definition of these words the following day, but only three out of the eight children understood '*most slippery*' and '*least slippery*'.

Figure 4.8 shows the children's abilty to give the correct definitions of the key vocabulary when they were asked in conversational contexts, the day after the experiments.

The vocabulary, *ramp, surface* and *slope,* associated with the car experiment, was demonstrated to the children. When asked to explain these words the next day, 'ramp' and 'slope' were consolidated for most children but only four out of eight could explain what a 'surface' was.

In the children's verbal explanations to the group, there was little evidence of the target vocabulary being used. Four children used no target vocabulary at all while the remaining four used one target word each – either 'smooth' or 'smoother'. The vocabulary used while the pupils were carrying out the experiment was not recorded. It would have provided contextually embedded language use and could have been contrasted with the decontextual language use of the key curriculum vocabulary. More information about pupils' use of language in learning would have been available to the teacher.

Non-curricular learning

Aim A: Work cooperatively with partner on car experiment
This aim directly encourages a Vygotskian approach to interactive learning. The children were allowed to choose their own partner to work with. Evaluation showed that five out of the group of eight pupils worked together and careful planning would be required for the remaining three. Two pairs worked cooperatively but only Peter and Simon worked as a team. Michael and Raymond took two sets of apparatus and each carried out a different part of the experiment but then tried to pool their results. They all achieved their individual targets. No one chose to work with Roger, the learner with the most substantial language difficulties, although Angela, with less difficulties, agreed to work with him. Despite Angela's attempts, Roger worked independently and disrupted the work of others so that he did not achieve his individual target of working cooperatively for ten minutes. Timothy and Jane did not engage in the experiment either and did not achieve their individual targets for this aim.

The main ways in which the evaluation from the first lesson influenced planning for the second session was through curriculum aims, presenting vocabulary, and cooperative learning.

Curriculum aims: Before the next lesson the teacher developed pupils' awareness of a 'fair test', through role play in a drama lesson. Also in preparation for the afternoon session, she revised on the morning of the lesson, weighing in grams and appropriate recording.

Presentation: To present the new target vocabulary the teacher made new flash cards with pictures and displayed them around the room. She produced a checklist for children to help them collect necessary equipment at the beginning of the experiment, and she linked it to the worksheet activity. The teacher amended the worksheet, adding visual clues to reflect two levels of cognitive demand, one with extension activities. She also became more conscious of her language of instruction.

Cooperative learning: To support the paired learning activity the teacher allocated the pupils' partners, by pairing a pupil who was able to do the maths involved with a partner who was less able. She paired children with similar scientific skills together to encourage equal interaction rather than the less scientifically-able being lead by their partner. The teacher and learning support assistant each took supervision of two pairs. This enabled them to have the time and space to focus on specific pupils, allowing them to observe, monitor and record four pupils learning. It also meant that the teacher relied on her colleague's notes to record the pupils' learning. They planned and agreed what they would record.

Evaluation of Lesson 1

In presenting their findings to the group, pupils would be encouraged first to draw the sequence of activities they did and then to use it as a 'prop' when talking. Each pupil would report back since they found it difficult to coordinate collaborative feedback in pairs. To reduce the time spent listening to others, the pupils would report in two groups to each adult. Pupils with difficulties attending would be given specific listening or questioning tasks, such as Roger asking one peer about his experiment.

Planning Lesson 2

The subsequent planning of the second lesson was based on the evaluation of Lesson 1. The long-term aims remained the same, however, the lesson aims for the second session are different although some aims in Science, and English are maintained, as well as the non-curricular aim. (See Figures 4.2, 4.3 and 4.4 for long-term aims.) Objectives for the second lesson are set out in Figure 4.9.

Individual aims for Lessons

Figure 4.10 shows the individual objectives planned for the session which differentiate the lesson aims described in Figure 4.9.

Teaching Lesson 2

The second Science session took place three weeks later, for an hour and a half in the afternoon, with the teacher and learning support assistant and eight pupils.

Lesson 2 objectives

Science

A   Gain an understanding of the importance of a strong structure
B   Carry out an experiment to investigate the strength of different structures
C   Say whether the test was fair/unfair
D   Measure accurately the weight load the bridge will hold
E   Measure accurately the 50 centimetres gap between tables
F   Say why one structure was stronger than another
G   To record results

English

A   Present findings to group verbally and explain what they did and why
B   To listen to each child present their findings
C   To carry out verbal and written instructions accurately
D   Check understanding and use of the following vocabulary:
    *bridge   strong   structure   gap   grams   right angle
    biggest weight   smallest weight*

Non-curricular

A   Work with partner on bridge experiment

Figure 4.9

The session started by introducing the eight target vocabulary words on flash cards and was followed by games to help the pupils identify the words, such as 'which word is missing'. The teacher walked with the pupils around the unit, identifying the building structures and talking about what made a structure strong.

The 'bridge challenge' was presented where the pupils had to make bridges spanning 50 centimetres from two cards, one of flat card and one with a right angled framework. They worked in pairs but this time they were told who their partner would be and which adult would be working with them. The teacher worked with Simon and Peter, and Roger and Jane, while the learning support assistant worked with Timothy and Angela, and Raymond and Michael. The task was planned to last about one hour.

Organisational support was given to start the task with a list of words and pictures of objects that each group needed to collect in order to do the experiment. When all items had been collected the pupils sat down in pairs while the teacher called out each item and one partner held up the item for checking.

When each pair had made the bridges, the pupils discussed in a group how to weight-test the bridges before doing it. They were shown where to record their results on their worksheet. The teacher and assistant checked the accuracy of the tests. The pupils drew quickly pictorial representations of what they had done in

Individual objectives

Name	Science	English	Non-curricular
Peter	A	A – without hesitations	A
	B	B	
	C – give 1 variable	C – no adult help	
	D	D – explain 6 target words	
	E	– use 3 target words	
	F – using word 'structure'		
	G – on his own		
Michael	A	A – without prompting	A
	B	B	
	C – give 1 variable	C – using visual clues	
	D	D – explain 7 target words	
	E	– use 3 target words	
	F – using word 'structure'		
	G – answers in correct place		
Roger	A	A – without hesitations	A – adult supervision
	B – with adult help	B – listen to 1 child	
	C – recognise 1 variable	C – using visual clues	
	D – with adult help	D – explain 4 target words	
	E	– use 1 target word	
	F – with prompting		
	G – answers in correct place		
Raymond	A	A – concisely	A
	B	B	
	C – give 1 variable	C – using visual clues	
	D	D – explain 8 target words	
	E	– use 3 target words	
	F – using word 'structure'		
	G – answers in correct place		

Figure 4.10 (*continued on next page*)

Individual objectives

Name	Science	English	Non-curricular
Angela	A	A – using 2 target words	A
	B	B	
	C – recognise 1 variable	C – no adult help	
	D – with adult help	D – explain 5 target words	
	E		
	F – with prompting	– use 3 target words	
	G – answers in correct place		
Jane	A	A – without hesitations	A – without dominating
	B – with adult help	B – without interrupting	
	C – recognise 1 variable	C – with visual clues	
	D – using word 'structure'	D – explain 8 target words	
	E		
	F	– use 3 target words	
	G – on her own		
Simon	A	A – confidently	A
	B – with adult help	B	
	C – give 1 variable	C – no adult help	
	D	D – explain 8 target words	
	E		
	F – using word 'structure'	– use 3 target words	
	G – answers in correct place		
Timothy	A	A –without hesitations	A – verbally
	B – with adult help	B	
	C – recognise 1 variable	C – using visual clues	
	D – with adult help	D – explain 6 target words	
	E		
	F – with prompting	– use 1 target word	
	G – answers in correct place		

Figure 4.10 (*continued*)

sequence, which each child used as support when reporting to their group about their findings.

Evaluation of Lesson 2

Evaluation of Lesson 2 is based on the modifications of Lesson 1 and information collected during the session from observations, discussion, tape recordings of explanation by pupils of their experiment and pupils' responses to questions the following day. The evaluations were recorded in curriculum notes on pupils' individual records and in pupils' Individual Educational Programmes completed at the end of term.

Understanding 'fairness'
The children enjoyed the drama session and were able to point out easily when a situation was fair or unfair, but the teacher was not sure of their understanding of a 'fair test' within the Science curriculum context. Five of the seven pupils displayed a greater awareness of a fair test in this second lesson, when asked how they made their experiment 'fair', while Roger and Angela showed no understanding of a fair test.

Revision of weighing
The pupils enjoyed estimating and weighing accurately in grams (in multiples of 10) and were confident when it came to testing their bridges. However, weight-testing the bridges was possibly successful because it was done as a class task. The pupils as a group counted together each 10 gram weight that was added on. They understood that the bridge which withstood the greatest weight was the strongest structure. By contrast, no child was able to explain this accurately and only five pupils referred to the weights as a measure of strength of structure.

Worksheet with visual clues
The revised format of the worksheet supported the pupils' recording. Pictures and target words in bold print referred the pupils to the relevant flash cards on display, which enabled them to complete the relevant answers in the correct place.

Drawing sequence of events as an aid to verbal reporting
This was an effective strategy. All the children managed to report on the experiment without teacher prompting. More targets were met in this area this time than in the previous lesson. Four pupils, Jane, Angela, Roger and Raymond, understood what they had to do and did it well. Peter and Simon drew the equipment they had used and labelled it while Timothy drew one picture of the whole experiment. The order for reporting individually also helped the pupils' organisation.

Shorter self-reporting time

Pupils listened attentively to each others' reports when placed in smaller groups. Roger who had had particular difficulties, was required to listen to one peer, attended for longer than in the last lesson and was able to give some feedback on Angela's experiment. Timothy was very dysfluent and the children in his group listened patiently. However, the teacher became aware that Timothy was not yet at the stage of giving an unaided verbal explanation.

Teacher's awareness of language of instruction

The teacher raised her awareness of her own language use through a conscious effort to use target words which reinforced the target vocabulary for the children. She found that her simplified instructions enhanced the pupils' understanding and there was less confusion on their part compared with the previous lesson. She noted that the instruction 'draw a sequence of pictures' was not understood by all pupils, and it would need to be clarified.

Checklist for pupils to collect necessary equipment

The list on the board worked well, apart from confusion over red card for the template, and a piece of card for cutting out strips. Verbal instructions also failed to clarify this confusion.

New vocabulary on flash cards

This was a successful support strategy. Flash cards were displayed on the board throughout the lesson as visual support to pupils' language. When new curriculum vocabulary was tested out of context the next day, 4 out of 7 children gave good definitions of all 8 target words. The other 3 pupils scored 7 out of 8, producing a higher success rate than in Lesson 1. This strategy also improved language use of target curriculum vocabulary. The verbal explanations in the second lesson of all pupils included at least one target word and 5 children used more than 1 target word, whereas in the first lesson, 4 children used no target vocabulary at all and the other 4 children only used 1 target word.

Interactive learning

The aim of working in pairs was to promote interactive learning and cooperation. Each group showed different levels of interaction. Only one group worked together on the bridge. The other pairs chose to make a bridge each. Examples from transcripts (see Figure 4.11) illustrate the quality and quantity of interactive learning going on. They show that using language as a tool for learning is not an easy option for pupils with language difficulties.

Example of working in pairs

Simon and Peter
Peter: 'I'll take a bit [masking tape] and then Simon can have the whole reel.'
However, Peter tended to speak to himself rather than to Simon: 'I'm going to plan it first and get it all set on the table.'

After 35 minutes Simon spoke to Peter, when he was asking for card. Simon: 'You can have some of mine.'

After an hour Simon had only made one side of his bridge and he said 'Peter'. Peter responded to this plea for help. Peter told him he had made the wrong shape and started taking off the middle bars. Simon was happy for Peter to do this.

Raymond
Raymond's partner was sick two minutes into the lesson and was sent home. Raymond could have joined another pair but he chose to work alone and was unable to achieve his targets of cooperation and interaction.

Figure 4.11

Adult supervision of the pupils
Allocating half the pupils to each member of staff for the whole lesson was a successful strategy. It enabled more detailed observation and recording by each adult of four pupils. The teacher also noted that her intervention and comments led to pupils attempting to resolve problems as they came to them. She was operating in the pupils' ZPD in interactive learning.

Some examples from transcripts illustrate the interaction (Figure 4.12). The teacher noted after doing the transcriptions that she had spent more of her time interacting with one pair.

Implications of the evaluation of Lesson 2

The evaluations of Lesson 2 indicated further learning and individual differentiation, such as working on tessellation, developing worksheets which differentiated on visual clues, encouraging pupils to work together rather than on different tasks and to try to resolve problems with their partner rather than waiting for an adult to intervene.

> **Interactive learning between pupils and teacher**
>
> Simon tried to span the gap by holding bits of card in place but without using masking tape. The teacher talked him through it and he said, 'I ought to stick it down'.
>
> Roger: 'You draw, I cut'. Jane did nothing while waiting and vice versa. When asked how they could make better use of their time, they did not answer but both got a piece of card and started making lots of strips.
>
> Jane was using thin, white card when the yellow card ran out. When asked if that was a good idea, she thought about it and said, 'No, it's too thin' and she went to change it.
>
> When Roger finished his flat bridge he just stood there. When the teacher asked him what he was going to do next, he said, 'I'll help Jane'.

Figure 4.12

Conclusion

This action research project has shown in some detail how the teacher set about reflecting on her planning and evaluation in one area of curriculum learning, with a group of pupils with speech and language difficulties. The nature of the support this group of pupils requires has been discussed, in terms of the planning and collaborative work among staff. Changes in how staff worked together were effective and are likely to continue, both at the level of classroom management and planning and evaluation.

The assessment process itself should not determine what is to be taught, nor be a 'bolt on' feature of classroom work. It should be an integral part of the educational process, providing both 'feedback' and 'feedforward'. The teacher in this study intends to extend an 'action research approach' to all areas of the curriculum as a means of supporting her teaching with this group of pupils, to enhance their learning and to work more collaboratively and effectively with her colleagues.

Chapter 5

Planning Modern Foreign Languages lessons

Introduction

This chapter looks at aspects of teaching French in a secondary special school. Until the mid 1980s, students in special schools had rather limited access to a curriculum in modern foreign languages (MFL). At best, some elements for example, of French language and culture, were built into a humanities module. In many cases, they were not taught at all. However, since September 1993, it has been statutory to teach a foreign language to all secondary-age students in England and Wales. The document, *Modern Foreign Languages for Ages 11 to 16* (Department of Education and Science/Welsh Office 1990) stated that all pupils, including those with special educational needs, should have the opportunity to experience a modern foreign language. Many teachers in mainstream and special schools expressed serious concern about the value and purpose of MFL teaching, especially to children who had profound or severe learning difficulties. Doubts, scepticism and perhaps anxiety were expressed by teachers who sometimes were concerned about whether children who were acquiring their first language only slowly could be expected to learn other languages (Veliante 1995). On the other hand, there were many MFL teachers who saw this change as a welcome and natural progression from the first introduction of the National Curriculum.

In the past, language courses may have been predominantly linked with examination requirements and pupils with special educational needs were often excluded. Ability in foreign languages was sometimes assumed to be demonstrated through vocabulary lists and grammatically correct, mainly written, structures. However, the document *Modern Foreign Languages in the National Curriculum* (Department for Education and Employment 1995d) suggests that the revised National Curriculum provides teachers with much greater flexibility to respond to the needs of pupils with identified special needs. However, considerable changes in thinking were necessary as teachers began to adapt and differentiate the MFL curriculum to meet the needs of all secondary-age students.

Why teach modern foreign languages?

The teaching of modern foreign languages raises a number of issues and, with particular reference to pupils with special educational needs, it is worth reviewing the aims of such teaching. As with the English curriculum, modern foreign language teaching has four broad Attainment Targets: listening, speaking, reading and writing. Activities would also have the following aims:

to develop the ability to use language effectively for purposes of practical communication;

to form a sound base of the skills, language and attitudes required for further study, work and leisure;

to offer insights into the culture and civilisation of the countries where the language is spoken;

to develop an awareness of the nature of language and language learning;

to provide enjoyment and intellectual stimulation;

to encourage positive attitudes to foreign languages and a sympathetic approach to other cultures and civilisations;

to promote learning of skills of more general application (e.g. analysis, memorising, drawing of inferences);

to develop pupils' understanding of themselves and their own culture.
(Department of Education and Science/Welsh Office 1990)

There are clear links between the learning of a first language and a 'foreign' language. The learning of foreign languages is thus an extension of children's learning of *language* and, as Lee (1991) observes, it engages intellectual, social, cultural and affective aspects of learning. In learning modern foreign languages, students become aware of the nature of language by experiencing, or by consciously thinking about, new language that is different from their own. It has the potential to enhance their awareness of many aspects of language and to enable pupils to manipulate and play with language in ways which may not be possible in their own, too familiar, language. The learning of a foreign language can help pupils to think differently about language and to talk about language. There may be opportunities to listen to sounds and rhythms that are different from those in their first language and to ask questions such as 'How do you say . . . in French?' 'What's the French for . . .?'. This so-called metalinguistic awareness, or the ability to think and talk about language, is considered to be an important aspect of development and in particular to assist in the development of literacy. It has the potential to enable a person to take greater control of language. This will be an important target for all children but will have particular significance for children with difficulties in language and communication.

A further, important feature of foreign language learning is the opportunity it provides for students to succeed. As a new subject for many students going into secondary school, they are unlikely to have experienced failure or poor achievement in a foreign language and there is therefore potential for raising pupils' self-esteem. Perhaps this is the primary aim of MFL teachers and, if self-esteem is linked with overall social and communication development, there can be no doubts about the rationale for this area of the curriculum.

Planning for effective MFL teaching

The planning of foreign language teaching will, clearly, require knowledge of the particular language. Where there are pupils with special educational needs, it will also be important to understand their specific strengths and needs. The linking of these two areas of teachers' knowledge and skill may be especially challenging and the support of colleagues can be particularly helpful. At times, it can be difficult for an individual practitioner to reflect critically and objectively on their own work. The reviewing process is enhanced if information can be discussed with a colleague or critical friend. In collaboration, professionals can contribute and gain new insights and as a result new plans can be devised and carried out. In many cases, collaboration between the specialist language teachers and the special educational needs coordinator, or another teacher or assistant who supports pupils with special needs, will provide the best opportunities for successful planning. Where there are children with particular language and communication difficulties, a speech and language therapist may also be involved. Successful collaboration inevitably takes time, to discuss and plan together and to ensure that everyone is able to contribute their views. In a study of schools which were introducing modern foreign languages to pupils with special educational needs it was recommended that teachers should be able to spend non-contact time together (Lee 1991). Without this, it was suggested that it would be difficult for colleagues to work in equal partnership with complementary skills and knowledge. Practitioners will have to consider carefully how this can be made possible and will need to enlist senior colleagues who can support their collaborative activities.

The planning

The plan and description of French teaching sessions which follow relate to a Year 10 class with 12 students, two of whom are described as having speech and language difficulties. The focus of teaching and learning is on realistic, active and practical communication, with greater emphasis on listening and speaking in the foreign language. The plan and subsequently the lesson, resulted from a group effort by staff. Their wish to critically analyse and evaluate their activities lead to a changed, improved lesson plan based on an adapted format. This forms part of a cycle where reflection on practice aims to continuously improve the quality of students' learning.

Assessment of students' learning and of teachers' teaching is an important component of the cycle. Teacher assessment needs to be preceded by careful planning followed by subsequent management of teaching stages, bearing in mind the students' individual needs. Assessment is effective when it leads to reflection on how and why things happened and on future action to improve existing teaching methods and students' learning. During this process of reviewing existing practice, clear, appropriate learning goals are established which form key elements in the planning of the next teaching sessions.

In working to include all pupils in classroom teaching and learning, teachers will face pupils in their class whose individual needs may be different from those of the majority of the class. Tried and tested teaching strategies may not have the usual effect. An action research approach can help in developing the reflective practice which can lead to greater understanding of pupils' individual needs.

This is particularly important when planning lessons for children with speech and language difficulties, who may not be able to pay attention or understand in the same way as other pupils. They may not be able to participate verbally to the same extent in lessons, or their contributions may be less intelligible. Class teachers of children with speech and language difficulties should expect to have regular meetings with learning support assistants (LSAs), parents, educational psychologists and speech and language therapists. All of these provide valuable information which can contribute to revised lesson plans of subsequent teaching sessions.

In the plans presented below, K and S are described as having speech and language difficulties. S had joined the class less than a week before recorded planning began. He had transferred from another secondary special school where MFL were not taught.

Notes made immediately after the session help in a subsequent evaluation and lead to changes which will be described. During the review, positive as well as negative aspects of teaching are considered. New targets are being set. A further MFL teaching session is planned and carried out for the same year group using the new lesson plan. The action research spiral has then completed one cycle and is ready to move forwards.

Planning the first lesson

The main aim of the MFL department is for students to enjoy the language and maintain their enthusiasm through focus on active communication, keeping the written element to a minimum. This enables students to experience and celebrate their own achievement, however small that may be. A learner-centred, communicative approach is used. The aim is to motivate students to want to learn the target language so that they will use it for their own purpose of communication.

Students in Years 10 and 11 at the school follow a French course consisting of self-contained modules lasting approximately four lessons (Bates *et al.* 1996). They are taught once a week for 40 minutes. The modules require students to have minimal previous knowledge of the foreign language. This is particularly appropriate, as many of the students experience memory difficulties. 'Long-term' aims are based on four-lesson blocks.

Long-term aims
Students to understand and practise new 'language of weather' module, in order to be able to take part in role play scenes.

Students to develop listening, speaking, reading and writing skills in French through focus on new 'language of weather' module (MFL National Curriculum Attainment Target (AT)1: Listening, AT 2: Speaking, AT 3: Reading and AT 4: Writing).

Learning tasks
1. To introduce new module, making clear aims and outcome of the module.
2. To introduce new weather vocabulary.
3. To develop listening skills: to show understanding of short French phrases placed in context; to respond to a clear model of standard French language spoken at reduced speed.
4. To develop speaking skills: to give short, simple responses in French; to describe pictures and objects with single French words using approximate pronunciation which is understandable by a sympathetic native speaker.
5. To develop reading skills: to show understanding of short familiar phrases presented in clear print; to match sound to print by reading aloud individual familiar words.
6. To prepare for learning homework of new phrases.
7. To develop social communication skills: to pay attention to speaker; to improve concentration; to show appropriate eye contact; to use appropriate turn-taking skills; to accept rules of a game; to show respect for each other.

Resources
The planning of any teaching and learning will need to take account of the effective use of resources, including the people available. In this case they were:

Learning Support Assistant
video
overhead projector (OHP)
tape recorder
flash cards
whiteboard
self-adhesive weather labels
worksheet
homework sheet.

Lesson outline

The outline of the lesson takes into account a range of objectives related to paying attention, listening, speaking and reading.

1. To introduce weather module, students watch a two-minute video of weather forecast; brief discussion, comparisons with own language, followed by demonstration of aims of module; recap principles of role plays.

2. To develop listening skills through presentation of weather vocabulary, show pictures on OHP, play tape recording of brief weather expressions, to be repeated at slower speed by teacher; match with pictures; similar matching activity, this time with coloured flash cards which, once core vocabulary is understood by most students, is turned into a team game; constantly attending to and stimulating students' attention skills as part of improving their listening skills through verbal as well as non-verbal reinforcers.

3. To develop speaking skills: hold up flash cards and say corresponding weather expression, students to repeat as a group, followed by volunteering individuals; for this, differentiation is by outcome, students either say initial sound, core word or the complete weather expression; this is turned into a guessing game where teacher initially whispers the new language, then just mouths it; next, students are not shown the picture on the flash card and have to guess it using taught French weather expressions; teacher to respond only with 'oui' or 'non'; if positive, student keeps the flash card; winner is the one with most flash cards.

4. To develop reading skills and prepare for learning homework, write and repeat verbally core words of weather expressions in large print on whiteboard; to match with self-adhesive weather labels; pointing at print and picture, hand out worksheet and read aloud together with class focusing on initial sounds of words, which are underlined; students have to fill in the missing words in part-printed weather expressions and draw the matching weather symbol; give out homework sheet which shows the complete weather phrases, used in previous listening and speaking activities, as well

as the same weather symbols as the ones used on the OHP and the self-adhesive labels; students copy the core words from the board in between the matching text and picture; differentiated learning homework consists of either learning the copied core words or the whole weather expressions.

Although not all pupils will perform in all skills, it is useful to identify general targets which will apply to all students. Deane (1992) suggests that minimum attainable targets are set. In this case they were:

to be able to understand some of the core language;
to be able to express verbally some of the core language;
to match some visual stimuli with some of the printed core language;
to copy some of the printed core language from the whiteboard;

With these general targets in mind, individual targets are also set so that each pupil will have a minimum to be attained. Individual targets for K and S were discussed with the LSA who would support them:

K – To note down initial letters of words from whiteboard, LSA to help with written work.
S – To develop expressive language skills by attempting initial sound of core expressions.

Using all of these considerations a plan was drawn up for the first of four teaching sessions (see Figure 5.1 at end of chapter, p. 79).

Evaluation of MFL lesson

Once the first lesson had taken place, the plan was discussed with a teacher colleague and the LSA in order to identify areas of strength and weakness. Using this first lesson as a basis, the aim was for future lesson plans to improve on this and for subsequent lessons to be more effective. Generally, it was considered that the plan formed a good base. However, it was noted that there was no place for some essential information in the existing lesson plan format. There was no mention of 'key vocabulary' or 'individual targets'. Communication between colleagues who were involved in the lessons was therefore inadequate. The plan was consequently developed and rewritten, based on the first lesson taught. (See Figure 5.2, p.80).

Some information, for example students' individual targets, needed to be more specific. Student K, after watching the introductory video, found it hard to focus on the discussion and perseverated loudly on presenters of British television weather forecasts. He gave detailed, but irrelevant information about Michael Fish and Susanne Charlton (television forecasters). It took a lengthy, quiet, one-to-one conversation with K and the prospect of obtaining the full merit mark at the end of the lesson, to bring him back to the task. Throughout the lesson, K displayed some repetitive behaviours such as hand-flapping and biting his index finger repeatedly. These behaviours were not mentioned in his individual targets, even though they occurred frequently when he became excited during games. They needed to be addressed as part of the overall plan to develop improved communication skills.

As colleagues discussed the experience of the lesson, ideas and comments were pooled, highlighting aspects which needed improvement. It was suggested that the class had been faced with too many weather expressions in one lesson. Only one out of 12 students remembered the English meaning of 'il fait du brouillard' (it is foggy) and it would possibly have been more beneficial to use fewer phrases. Instead, there could be more repetition or consolidation through a wider variety of activities.

The biggest challenge was presented by S, who had only recently joined the school and took part in his first ever French lesson. The teacher knew he had some difficulties expressing himself, but was unaware of the extent of the problem and the direct effect it would have on his spoken communication. S tried to produce initial sounds of words, for example, 's' for 'sun' which he accompanied with sign language. Even though he obviously wanted to participate, his attempts were largely unintelligible to everyone. In addition, he could not read words printed on the whiteboard or on worksheets.

A meeting between the speech and language therapist, LSA and teacher was arranged prior to the next French lesson. It became evident that some of the records from his last school had not been passed on. The therapist, who had known him in his previous school, was able to provide important information and to suggest strategies. S had a visual impairment which required print to be enlarged and placed on a slightly tilted board on top of his desk. S's difficulties in producing speech sounds were partly caused by a condition which severely disrupted the motor control of his speech. When he attempted to produce an initial sound, he used either the British finger spelling alphabet or a symbol from Paget Gorman Signed Speech which he was taught at his previous school. This seemed to offer a useful way to enhance his communication. The principles of the finger spelling were explained by the speech and language therapist and guidelines were handed out to all colleagues.

Colleagues' observations suggested that the range of activities and diversity of strategies were successful in the first lesson. These had helped the students to achieve their general targets. Focusing on initial letter sounds in listening and reading activities appeared to have helped the students to memorise new language. The games had clearly motivated the students, who could easily have continued with those until the end of the lesson.

The observed highlights and weaknesses of the lesson were summarised.

Strengths

1. The video presented a stimulating start to the module; it encouraged group discussion.
2. The variety of activities helped to maintain the students' attention. Their enthusiasm lasted for most of the lesson. They responded with positive feedback at the end of the lesson: 'That lesson went quick, wicked!'
3. Focus on initial letter sounds was successful in both listening and reading activities.
4. The games were a great success.
5. All general targets were met.

Weaknesses

1. The planned role play did not present an appropriate long-term goal; it was too vague and artificial.
2. Too much new language was presented at once.
3. The pace of presentation was too fast.
4. Not all students' needs were taken into account; not all of their individual targets were specified, for example, some quiet students could have been encouraged to contribute more.
5. The literacy worksheet was too demanding; the majority of students seemed tired and experienced difficulties.
6. Student K did not stay focused and showed signs of repetitive behaviours; individual targets were too vague and should have been more clearly defined, for example, for K to stay focused for a specified amount of time.
7. S could not read presented print; he had major problems expressing himself due to unforeseen, severe difficulties with speech sounds.

Revised planning and effects of subsequent MFL lesson

The planning of any lessons needs to take account of the individual strengths and needs of the children and an understanding of the way each child responds will be important. Where children have speech and language difficulties, account will be taken of the specific nature of their difficulty. To be able to reflect on existing practice and adapt strategies according to the students' needs is central to achieving effective teaching and is, of course, the essence of differentiation.

The development of suitable teaching and learning activities must always be open to change in the light of experience and new information. The employment of a cycle of planning, acting and reflecting can lead to change and improvement in existing practice. In this case, the cycle suggests how a further MFL lesson which followed the revised lesson plan, could result in more effective teaching and improve students' learning, as it was based on insights and conclusions drawn from the evaluation of a lesson plan and the experience of teaching the lesson.

A new plan was drawn up, using the experience of the previous lessons, for the first of four more teaching sessions. The title of the new module was 'At the Post Office' (see Figure 5.3 p.81).

Generally, most of the methods and approaches applied in the first lesson were appropriate. The choice and management of activities were also considered to be suitable. They could therefore be adopted again in subsequent lessons. They had helped to achieve the main aims which were to make MFL learning an enjoyable experience, to foster active communication in the foreign language and, as a consequence it was hoped that students' self-esteem would be raised.

Discussions with colleagues and further reviews had helped to identify areas which could be improved. The focus had shifted from a general MFL lesson plan to one which took account of the specific needs of individual students, including those with speech and language difficulties.

The selection and amount of new vocabulary needed reviewing. Many children with speech and language difficulties do not learn language easily or spontaneously and possibly, some do not learn language in the same way as their peers. The introduction of new vocabulary has to be carefully planned. Consideration needs to be given to the number of new words and phrases. These may have to be repeated regularly and in many different ways. Different pupils will learn in different ways, that is, they have different 'learning styles'. For example, some may be helped by visual material and others by auditory stimuli. Some learn better individually, while others respond to questions and discussion in groups. It is important, when working with a group, to utilise a range of approaches in order to meet the preferred learning style of all pupils. Conversely, when working with individuals, it is important that they experience a variety of approaches in order to develop a wider repertoire of learning strategies (Kyriacou et al. 1996).

In the new plan for At the Post Office, fewer words and phrases were introduced. Students were therefore able to memorise almost all of the new language, even though one of them required some visual prompting (holding up a stamp when 'un timbre' was the required response). The students' memory of the newly-taught core words was assessed during listening activities in both lessons. Comparison of the two charts (Figures 5.4 and 5.5 p.82/83) show that students had a higher success rate in the second lesson (the 'post office' lesson) compared with those of the first (the 'weather' lesson).

Additionally, the new vocabulary was carefully selected for practical reasons. It could easily be connected to create a range of simple, realistic role play situations at the post office. All students, including the shy ones, had an opportunity to practise and adapt newly-learned language in pairs. They enjoyed this social learning activity, especially as real props, such as stamps, postcards and envelopes were used. It was anticipated however, that student K might be distracted by these props. He was therefore placed with a role play partner close to a support assistant. She occasionally redirected him back to the task as he tried to divert the conversation to his brother's stamp collection. However, when compared with the previous lesson, this did not interfere with the continuity and progression of the class as a whole and his diversions did not last as long.

Target setting for individual students had to be further improved. Clearly defined, realistic, mostly short-term targets were set for both students K and S. Some of these had been previously discussed with teacher, students, parents and LSA and recorded on the students' Individual Education Programmes. It was agreed that a consistent adult approach was important.

Student K needed support in remaining on task. His target, which was discussed with him, was to stay focused for a minimum of, initially, one minute, when addressed personally. On successful completion, this would be gradually increased. Apart from digressing on to his brother's stamps, he did succeed in meeting this specific target. His hand-flapping and finger-biting were also addressed. In order to raise his awareness of these behaviours, they were discussed with him during lunchtime. He agreed to follow a staged plan which should help him first to reduce hand-flapping, so that his behaviour would become more socially acceptable. Figure 5.6 (p.84) shows the plan, which was successful up to stage 4.

Student S had difficulties expressing himself verbally and communicating with his peers. As a result of a meeting between the teacher, LSA and S, it was agreed, at the boy's request, that he should use the British Finger Spelling Alphabet for initial letters in lessons and to attempt the initial letter sounds. This worked with limited success as his communication was restricted to single words. S stated that he preferred not to use Paget Gorman Signed Speech. Possibly at the age of fifteen he did not want to be seen to be very different from his friends. Communication with his peers remained difficult, even though it slowly improved as other students began to learn finger spelling, displayed near the whiteboard and his desk.

Children with speech and language difficulties may experience additional problems. Written language is closely linked with spoken language and many children with speech and language difficulties also experience problems with literacy. They may also experience difficulties with their fine and/or gross motor control. K's letter formation was slow. His writing appeared large, unconnected and sometimes reversed. It seemed uncoordinated and was difficult to read. He held pens with a tight grip. However, as K's spelling and general reading ability were now in line with that of the rest of his peers, he was given access to a word-processing package on the computer. This greatly assisted and improved the presentation of his written work.

Additionally, K had difficulties with language meaning. He often made literal interpretations which suggested a difficulty in understanding that words can have more than one meaning. This sometimes made him appear bizarre or even rude. When the teacher explained to the students 'The core words are the ones in bold print', K responded: 'That's not right. How can words be bold. People are bold, aren't they?' The LSA managed to explain that the core words were in a darker, slightly bigger print. The teacher made an effort in the second lesson to avoid or to explain ambiguous language. Adults' language in class is an important element of differentiation. Close observation and comment by colleagues can be used to draw attention to style of presentation of information so that misunderstandings can be reduced. Forward planning will also help in identifying potential pitfalls so that explanations can be given and pupils can be helped to understand new language.

For student S, texts in all subsequent lessons were placed on a board, at an angle on top of his desk. They were enlarged and presented in clear print which contained essential, unambiguous information. This gave S the opportunity to respond more easily to written language.

Once the second lesson had been taught, the teacher, as well as the students, experienced a greater sense of achievement compared with the previous lesson. However, in reflecting on aspects of the second lesson, further areas for development could still be identified. It was noted that individual target setting could be extended and that the LSA could have been involved more effectively.

The spirals of planning, acting and reviewing can go on and on and can continue to influence change and further improvement. For any teaching it is impossible to foresee every eventuality. Each lesson will contain an unpredictable element. Changes can occur at many different levels. An approach which has been a real success for many classes, for some reason may not work. These are minor setbacks and should not divert from the main goals.

In addition to identifying pupils' needs, the reflective cycle can also raise issues for further staff development. For example, where aspects of further fine-tuning in lesson plans and activities are identified, staff may wish to consider the implications for their own professional learning. Does it mean that some further reading could be useful? Does it mean that discussion with a more experienced colleague, perhaps an 'outsider', could be useful? In the cycles described in this chapter, one of the conclusions was that some in-service training could be helpful.

Conclusion

The MFL department's main purpose was to boost students' self-confidence by giving them the opportunity to experience and to celebrate their own achievement. Pupils may easily dismiss their chances of success in learning a MFL, particularly when the criteria for success seem to mirror those on which they have been judged to have failed elsewhere, that is, in language. In guidance on modern foreign languages (National Curriculum Council 1992a), it is recommended that pupils should be able to take risks in a secure environment and experience success. A secure environment for students with special educational needs should certainly be attainable for the planning and teaching of MFL. It has the potential to offer a fresh start to pupils who might have experienced failure in their primary education, perhaps particularly those with speech and language difficulties. Students who experience literacy problems may find that they manage reading and writing activities in MFL. Students who find it difficult to talk in front of the class, may develop greater confidence through practice in role plays.

The SCAA (1997) publication, *Use of Language: a common approach*, recommends taking account of the needs of all pupils, including the more able, those with special educational needs and pupils for whom English is an additional language. The experiences described in this chapter suggest that this is possible in the case of modern foreign language teaching.

Figure 5.1 Lesson plan

Teacher _____   French   Year 7 8 9 10 11

Date 6 May 1997   Range within setting L 3   M 5   H 4   NC Levels W 1 2 3 4

Long-term aim
Students to understand and practise new language of weather module in order to actively participate in rehearsed role play.

Link to previous lesson: Yes   No

Learning Tasks	Minutes	Resources	ATs		Levels	Mode
Elicit information from video clip on weather forecast Group discussion and comparisons to own language Aims of module Recap principles of role play scenes	10 5	video	1 3	2 4	N/A	(i / p / g)
Introduce weather vocabulary, **develop** listening and speaking skills through range of activities and team games as well as games with individual winners	15	OHP tape recorder flash cards	1 3	2 4	1–2	(i / p / g)
Develop reading skills through whole group activity Read aloud as class and as individual Prepare for learning homework, copy **core** words from whiteboard	10	whiteboard; self-adhesive weather pictures; worksheet; homework sheet	1 3	3 41	1	(i / p / g)

Homework type   AT2 AT3 AT4, other – to learn eight new weather expressions
Differentiated homework – to focus on **core** words only

Time for individual assessment 5 minutes

SSA/other support present   Yes   No

Task: to assist with written activities

Areas of Experience   A. Everyday Activities
                         B. Personal & Social Life
                         C. The World around us
D. The World of Work
E. The World of Communication
F. The International World

Key: L = low; M = middle; H = high
      Ats = Attainment Targets – AT1 Listening; AT2 Speaking; AT3 Reading; AT4 Writing
      Mode: i = individual; p = pairwork; g = group

Figure 5.2 Revised lesson plan

Write only as much as is useful. You could use the back for your preparation notes and/or for your evaluation of how the lesson and the previous homework went.

Teacher _____ French   Year 7 8 9 10 11

Date 6 May 1997   Range within setting L 3   M 5   H 4   NC Levels W 1 2 3 4

Long-term aim: To understand and practise new language of weather module in order to take part in role play scenes; to focus on active communication through developing listening and speaking skills.

Short-term aims: To introduce new module with relevant weather vocabulary; to show understanding of heard and seen short weather phrases; to be able to give short, simple responses in French describing weather symbols using approximate pronunciation; to develop social communication skills in a range of structured situations.

Learning Tasks for lesson 1 out of 4	Key Vocabulary	Resources	ATs	Levels	Mode
Elicit information from *video* clip on weather forecast Group discussion and comparisons with British weather forecasts Present aims of module Recap principles of role play scenes	Bonjour la classe Asseyez-vous Silence Regardez la télé la **météo**	video	1 2 3 4	N/A	
Introduce weather vocabulary; develop listening and speaking skills through range of activities and team games as well as games with individual winners	il **pleut** il fait **chaud** il fait **froid** il fait du **vent** il fait du **soleil**	OHP1 tape recorder flash cards	2 3 4	1–2	
Develop speaking skills through differentiated group activity, say phrase aloud as class or as individual; hand out learning homework sheet, focusing on initial letters of **core** words	as in section above; au revoir	white board; self-adhesive weather pictures; homework sheet	1 2 3 4	1	

SSA/ other support: _____ Yes No   Homework type   AT2 AT3 AT4, other – to learn five new weather expressions

Task: to assist named students with agreed individual targets   Differentiated homework – to focus on **core** words

Individual Targets for **K:** interactional; to maintain appropriate non-verbal listening skills when spoken to and to stay focused for a minimun of 5 minutes; for **S:** to develop expressive language skills by attempting to say initial sounds; to present with texts in large print.

Key: L = low; M = middle; H = high
Ats = Attainment Targets – AT1 Listening; AT2 Speaking; AT3 Reading; AT4 Writing
Mode: i = individual; p = pairwork; g = group

Figure 3.3 New lesson plan – At the Post Office

Teacher _____   French   Year 7 8 9 10 11

Date 10 June 1997   Range within setting L 3   M 5   H 4   NC Levels W 1 2 3 4

Long-term aim: to develop French listening, speaking and writing skills through focus on new language of post office module in order to be able to buy stamps and postcards in France; to obtain RSA statement

Short-term aims: to introduce new module with relevant post office vocabulary; to show understanding of heard and seen short post office words and phrases; to be able to give short, simple responses in French in post office situations using approximate pronunciation; to develop social communication skills in a range of structured situations.

Learning Tasks for lesson 1 out of 4	Key Vocabulary	Resources	ATs		Mode
Introduction of module through group discussion about purpose of British post office as main stimulus Explain long-term aims	Bonjour la classe Asseyez-vous Silence Ecoutez! Regardez!	Flash cards	1 3	2 4	
Introduce part of post office vocabulary, develop listening skills through range of activities including various games with whole group as well as individuals	où est la poste? Voilà Merci Un timbre pour une carte postale/une lettre en Angleterre s'il vous plaît	OHP tape recorder flash cards	1 3	2 4	
Develop both listening and speaking skills through structured role plays, first with LSA as a model, then in pairs and Give out (learning) homework sheet and explain, focusing on initial letters of core words	All of the above and au revoir	post cards envelopes stamps homework sheet	1 3	2 3	

SSA/ other support: _____   Yes   No

Task: to assist named students with agreed individual targets

Homework type   AT2 AT3 AT4, other – to learn new post office expressions and revise previously taught phrases
Differentiated homework – to focus on 4 **core** words

Individual Targets for K: interactional; to maintain appropriate non-verbal listening skills when spoken to and to stay focused for a minimum of 1 minute; to follow staged plan to modify non-verbal behaviour patterns; to have access to a computer in activities which require written output; for **S:** to develop expressive language skills by saying initial sounds accompanied by signing; to have access to texts in large print.

Key: L = low; M = middle; H = high
Ats = Attainment Targets – AT1 Listening; AT2 speaking; AT3 Reading; AT4 Writing;
Mode: i = individual; p = pairwork; g = group

Use the Target Language for Real Purposes

Figure 5.4

La Météo

Students	Skill (AT1) Listening 1 6.5.97	2	Skill (AT2) Speaking 1 6.5.97	2 6.5.97	Skill (AT3) Reading 1 6.5.97	2	Skill (AT4) Writing 1	2
1. K.	70		✓	✓	✓			
2. S.	40		✓*	✓	✓*			
3. N.	70		✓		w			
4. I.	90		✓	✓	✓			
5. B.	A		A	A	A			
6. R.	70		✓	✓	w			
7. G.	80		✓	✓	✓			
8. D.	60		✓		✓			
9. A.	20		w		w			
10. W.	30		✓		w			
11. Y.	20		w		w			
12. T.	80		✓	✓	✓			

Key to Attainments

AT1, 1 Student is able to identify heard weather expression by matching them with relevant pictures/flash cards.

AT2, 1 Student is able to describe verbally a range of weather cards using taught core words; *student S is able to express initial sound of core words holding up matching weather card.

AT2, 2 Student is able to do above, plus using short phrases with approximate pronunciation.

AT3, 1 Student is able to match print with sound by reading aloud single words presented in clear print; *student S as in AT2, 1.

Figure 5.5

A la poste

Level: Date: Students	Skill (AT1) Listening 1 10.6.97	2 10.6	Skill (AT2) Speaking 1 10.6	2 10.6	Skill (AT3) Reading 1	2	Skill (AT4) Writing 1	2
1. K.	100	✓	✓	✓				
2. S.	80	✓	✓*					
3. N.	80		✓	✓				
4. I.	100	✓	✓	✓				
5. B.	80	✓	✓					
6. R.	80		✓	✓				
7. G.	100	✓	✓	✓				
8. D.	80	✓	✓					
9. A.	40		w					
10. W.	80		✓					
11. Y.	20		w					
12. T.	100	✓	✓	✓				

Key to Attainments

AT1, 1 Student is able to identify heard post office language by matching it with relevant pictures/flash cards.
AT2, 1 Student is able to respond to role play situations, shows understanding of short, rehearsed phrases.
AT2, 2 Student is able to describe verbally a range of post office words using relevant core words; *student S can say initial sound and match cards.
AT3, 1 Student is able to carry out AT2, 1; plus can participate in short, guided role play situations using memorised language with approximate pronunciation.

Student: K

Class: 10.2

Target: to reduce arm/hand-flapping behaviour by following a staged plan.

Aims: to stop arm/hand-flapping; to become less obtrusive to peers and self; to focus on topic; to conform with class and become socially acceptable.

Stage 1   When wanting to flap arms/hand, do so but modify slightly by holding the arms lower down in a less pronounced way

by: 20 May 1997   ☐

Stage 2:   On successful completion of Stage 1, when wanting to flap hand/arm, do so but modify above stage and flap hands just below the table

by: 3 June 1997   ☐

Stage 3: on successful completion of Stage 2, when wanting to flap hands, do so but modify above stage by flapping/moving just the fingers out of sight of others

by: 10 June 1997   ☐

Stage 4: on successful completion of Stage 3, when wanting to flap hands, do so but modify above stage and just move thumbs out of sight

by: 17 June 1997   ☐

Stage 5: on successful completion of Stage 4, when wanting to flap hands, look around at others and copy what they are doing (e.g. laughing and enjoying the situation)

by: 24 June 1997   ☐

I agree to the above plan and I will try to follow it: ....

(Student's signature)

Date: 7 May 1997

This plan is supported by:

(Parent) .... (LSA) .... (Teacher) ....

Figure 5.6

Chapter 6

Therapists and teachers collaborating in Science

Introduction

Cooperation and collaboration between adults in education can be productive, not only for children's learning but for the developments which can occur in adults' thinking. Team work can provide several points of view, shared problem-solving and mutual support. Where there are children with special educational needs, teachers, learning support assistants and other educational practitioners frequently work together. The education of pupils with speech and language difficulties requires two distinctive professions, teachers and speech and language therapists, to work collaboratively and regularly together. In this chapter, an action research approach was used to evaluate the work of a speech and language therapist in a Science class for children with specific language impairment. The succession of planning, action and evaluation stages enabled the therapist to analyse both the learning outcomes for individual children and the efficacy of her participation in the class. The project demonstrates how differentiation by language and by grouping of children can be used for effective teaching and learning.

Teachers and therapists in partnership

The Royal College of Speech and Language Therapists, the professional body for speech and language therapists, is very specific in its professional guidelines:

> Joint assessment, planning and intervention is seen as essential in meeting the needs of the child

> The programme of [speech and language therapy] intervention for the school aged child will be seen as part of his/her total education programme . . .
> (Royal College of Speech and Language Therapists 1996, p. 175)

Although speech and language therapists are not always considered to be educational practitioners, their work is expected to be well integrated with the curriculum.

There is increased interest in collaborative practice. In recent years a number of authors have attempted to identify features of effective collaboration and some of the particular barriers when teachers and speech and language therapists attempt to work together. McCartney and Van der Gaag (1996) note that some of the difficulties arise because the two groups of professionals come from different backgrounds and have different employers, the health and education services. They emphasise the importance of teachers and therapists sharing and understanding each others' point of view and in particular of speech and language therapists being able to identify their role in educational contexts. In our earlier publication (Martin and Miller, 1996) we too suggested that a more integrated approach would come from a sharing of perspectives on speech and language difficulties by teachers and speech and language therapists.

Exactly how therapists organise their work in a class and the ways in which they participate in the curriculum depends on a number of factors. In practice it is often determined by considering the needs of the children, the time available and the styles of working of individual class teachers and therapists.

Language and science

For most children, language is an important vehicle for teaching and learning. However, when children have language and communication difficulties, this can not be assumed. It may be necessary to teach directly the language they will need for learning in a particular curriculum area. In this way, the curriculum becomes a vehicle for the teaching of language. The teaching of science can be effective in developing language but there are potential pitfalls and planning will need to take account of a number of factors. All subjects have their own vocabulary and terminology. Indeed, groups of professionals may be accused of using 'jargon' when they use words in particular ways which only they understand for discussion of their subject. Science and scientists are no exception. Bulman (1985) discusses the teaching of language for studying science and points out that 'scientific language strives to be precise' (p. 21). There are therefore challenges for teachers and for pupils in mastering the precise meanings of words in science, which may differ from the ways in which these words are used in everyday activities. Anticipation of vocabulary and other aspects of the language to be used will form an important part of lesson planning.

Language will provide a tool for the teaching and learning of science and in particular, speaking and listening will be used for explanation and exploration of ideas. The encouragement of 'pupil talk' is important as it can increase their understanding of scientific concepts. Whereas more advanced pupils may 'rework' ideas 'in their heads' and will plan and write essays to develop their thoughts, for other pupils, most of the time this exploration 'will be done only through talk' (Bulman, p. 115). For pupils with language difficulties or other learning difficulties, exploration through talk may not always be possible and other approaches to the development of their understanding will be needed. In these cases, the presentation of concrete examples and participatory activities will assume special relevance. Further, as retention and memory may be weaker in these children, tasks will need to be repeated in a variety of ways which are meaningful and related to everyday experience if children are to actively engage with them.

Science for children with language difficulties

In the special school where this project took place, science teaching was organised in termly topics with a strong emphasis on vocabulary and language concept development. It was already recognised that the therapist had a role in the teaching of science topics and she was involved in the selection of appropriate vocabulary lists for the topic. She assessed the children's knowledge pre- and post-topic and was timetabled to be in the class during the science lessons.

Previously the therapist had worked with various groups of children in these lessons. Frequently, these were children thought to need more language support than a classroom assistant could give. The selection of childen was usually decided by the teacher or therapist at the start of the lesson and was not part of a plan for the term. The therapist felt that although her skills were being used, this arrangement was not entirely satisfactory. She had limited involvement in the planning for differentiation and was not able to maintain consistent records of progress for individual children. One aspect of this study therefore was to organise the children into small groups for science which would work together each time. The therapist would work with one group throughout the term. The second aspect was to observe how the children responded to the teaching activities and to establish to what extent learning of target words occurred.

The planning stage

The topic for the term was called 'All around us' and had a geography and science focus. For the purposes of this study the science element alone is considered, although the checklists used for assessments (see Figure 6.1) also show some of the geography vocabulary.

The topic incorporated aspects of Key Stages 1 and 2 of Science in the National Curriculum (Department for Education 1995b). The children were all within the Key Stage 2 age group, 7 to 11 years, but their different levels of ability meant

Group 1	Group 2
Spring	temperature
Summer	shade
Autumn	rainforest
Winter	desert
shadow	shadow
liquid	solid
sunny	
windy	liquid
rainy	
cloudy	
stormy	
snowy	

Figure 6.1 Checklist

that it was necessary to have regard for both Key Stages when planning the topic. The study, of 'Changing materials' formed the basis of the topic. Special attention was also given to the Programmes of Study at both Key Stages since the children being taught needed extra help with the items such as *systematic enquiry* and *communication* which depend strongly on language.

The two class teachers involved in teaching this topic and the therapist who worked with both of them met to plan for the term. The teachers identified the main activities which needed to be carried out and together, specific items of comprehension were agreed as suitable for measuring the children's pre-topic knowledge. From these responses appropriate targets for each child could be set. Their progress would then be checked using the same assessment at the end of term.

The children were asked 'concept questions' to assess their descriptions of their observations. Group 1's questions were largely based on their direct experiences and observations in activities, whereas children in Group 2 were expected to assimilate information from a number of sources in order to formulate a response. (See Figure 6.2.)

Assessment sheets for the children were devised showing the scientific focus (key concepts) of the topic. (See Figure 6.3, relating to Child 1 to Child 5.) The therapist was interested in the results from the group of children with severe language difficulties. They showed the limitations of the children's understanding and language skills when they were asked to describe what they observed. Their responses also raised the question 'how much can the children learn from science lessons?'.

With the teacher's agreement, the speech and language therapist chose to work with this group for the term's science lessons. There were children in the class with considerably higher levels of comprehension and several of them were experiencing some of their lessons in mainstream schools. The teachers

Group 1	Group 2
What happens when water gets very cold?	What is the weather like? (use of . . . y)
What happens if you take a lolly out in the sun?	Name the seasons of the year.
What happened to the Plasticine? (Changed shape)	What is a drought?
What happened to the teddies? (Changed colour)	What is a flood?
	What does 'tropical' mean?
	(a) What is ice?
	(b) How do you change it back to water?

Figure 6.2 Concept questions

welcomed the opportunity to concentrate on these children during science lessons. They suggested that one classroom assistant should permanently work with the therapist's group. This person had considerable experience with one of the children in the group whose behaviour and cooperation were unpredictable. The assistant would be able to give additional support to that child when required.

The activities planned by the teachers for the science lessons were to be basically the same for all the groups. However, there would be differentiation between the groups in terms of language used by the adult, responses expected from the children and method of recording used by the children. The children in

Key concepts   **Child 1**

Concept question	Pre-topic date 9/96	Post-topic date
What happens when water gets very cold?	raining	
What happens if you take a lolly out in the sun?	off my coat	
What happened to the Plasticine? (Changed shape)	it big it gone ball	
What happened to the teddies? (Changed colour)	teddy teddy	

Figure 6.3 (continued overleaf)

Key concepts   **Child 2**

Concept question	Pre-topic date 9/96	Post-topic date
What happens when water gets very cold?	it will get cold it will drop	
What happens if you take a lolly out in the sun?	it will melt	
What happened to the Plasticine? (Changed shape)	it's like a doughnut	
What happened to the teddies? (Changed colour)	yellow teddy bears	

Key concepts   **Child 3**

Concept question	Pre-topic date 9/96	Post-topic date
What happens when water gets very cold?	because it's very cold feeling cold	
What happens if you take a lolly out in the sun?	because it's getting sun	
What happened to the Plasticine? (Changed shape)	it's thunder it's getting stick	
What happened to the teddies? (Changed colour)	yellow	

Key concepts   **Child 4**

Concept question	Pre-topic date 9/96	Post-topic date
What happens when water gets very cold?	snow	
What happens if you take a lolly out in the sun?	summertime ice cream	
What happened to the Plasticine? (Changed shape)	it's raining and snowy thunder	
What happened to the teddies? (Changed colour)	yellow sun	

Figure 6.3 (continued)

90

Key concepts   **Child 5**

Concept question	Pre-topic date 9/96	Post-topic date
What happens when water gets very cold?	raining	
What happens if you take a lolly out in the sun?	in the beach	
What happened to the Plasticine? (Changed shape)	oh longer sausages	
What happened to the teddies?(Changed colour)	now blue teddy bears	

Figure 6.3 Concepts

the group led by the therapist could understand short sentences related to familiar situations. They could be expected to respond using single-word or short-phrase utterances. They would record their responses by drawing pictures in sequence, in prepared boxes in their books. Two children were able to write a few words to accompany each picture. The other three could copy-write or have their comments on each picture scribed by an adult.

The therapist planned and evaluated each lesson weekly. The teachers, therapist and two classroom assistants discussed the responses of all of the children informally at the end of each lesson.

The children

The five children in the therapist's group were aged between eight and ten years. They had all attended the school for two years or more and records showed that they all had ahistory of severe developmental language impairment. Four of the children presented additional social and behavioural difficulties associated with features of the autistic continuum. All were able to participate in small-group activities, being able to take turns and attend to what an adult in the group was doing. They all required some amount of support for this from an adult who could structure the turn-taking and redirect their attention as necessary. Although able to give visual attention to an adult in a group, the children were at different levels of ability to listen and would all need individual instructions from the adults in order to carry out a task.

In the pre-topic tests (see above) only Child 4 appeared to understand the question 'What happens when water gets very cold?' by responding 'snow'. Children 1 and 5 responded 'raining' which may mean that they were associating *water* and *cold*; children 2 and 3 repeated the question in some way.

Child 2 was the only one who correctly replied 'it will melt' to the question 'What happens if you take a lolly out in the sun?'. All of the others gave responses in some way associated with the word 'sun'.

The two other questions followed a short demonstration by the adult in which the children were asked to close their eyes while the adult effected a change on some Plasticine, then on two plastic bears. The aim was to allow the child to describe change. None of the children used the word 'change' although all described in some way the change that had occurred. Child 1, 2 and 3 used verbs to describe the Plasticine:

'it gone ball'
'it's like a doughnut'
'it's getting stick'.

Child 4 appeared to be still focused on recent questions about the weather, which may have been a sign of poor comprehension but he did refer to the bear's change of colour:

'yellow sun'.

Child 5 gave the most syntactically complete descriptions:

'oh longer sausages'
'now blue teddy bears'.

The children had all shown ability to *recognise change* but none of them had used the word spontaneously. The therapist therefore decided that the emphasis in science for the term would be for the children to learn the word 'change' and its various uses in everyday language. The understanding of this concept is fundamental to the understanding of the other concepts assessed: freezing and melting.

Aims and content of the lessons

The major long-term aims for this group were:

To understand the concept of *change* in relation to common events.
To use the word *change* when describing a simple event.

Six lessons to specifically address these aims were identified. The aims (learning outcome) and content (activity) of each of these are described below.

The school used the Paget Gorman Signing System and so this was used to support the spoken word during all lessons. Particular emphasis and repetition of the sign for 'change' was used.

Six lessons were planned which had the concept 'change' as a central theme.

The lessons were based on activities and the language of the lessons was carefully controlled by the therapist. Each lesson focused on the idea of 'change' through a different activity.

Lesson 1

Learning outcome: To respond *yes* or *no* to the statement
   water changes: flour, salt, sand, soil, stone, sugar.

Activities:
1. Identify the six substances with the children.
2. Take turns to add water and comment on any *change*.
3. Children draw each substance in their books and write a label if able.
4. Adult asks child to name each picture and after each one asks: 'Water changes (....................)?'. The child's response is written in their book.

Lesson 2

Learning outcomes:
1. To observe the changes involved in making jelly.
2. To draw four stages of the process.
3. To describe the four pictures to an adult.

Activities:
1. Make jelly, talking about each stage and letting each child have a turn.
2. Children to be given individual explanation of what to do in each box in their books.
3. Each child asked to describe their pictures and their words are written in their books by themselves or the adult.

Lesson 3

Learning outcome: To understand that 'water changes into ice'.

Activities:
1. Talk about the ice tray and what to put in it.
2. Children put water in it and put it in the freezer.
3. Next day look at the ice. Talk about *change*.
4. Leave a piece in the classroom to melt. Talk about *change*.

Lesson 4

Learning outcome: To use the phrase 'change colour' when making coloured icing.

Activities:
1. Make icing together.
2. Add food colouring. Talk about *change*.
3. Spread on biscuits.
4. Children to record in four pictures in their books.

5. Adult to use their pictures to ask 'what happens to the icing?'.
6. Eat biscuits!

Lesson 5

Learning outcome: To observe and describe the changes involved in making chocolate crispies.

Activities:
1. Children to take turns to break chocolate, stir it as it melts, add crispies and put into paper cases. Adults to encourage talk about what is happening.
2. Children to record the four stages in their books, with pictures and writing by themselves or by telling an adult.

Lesson 6

Learning outcome: To observe and talk about the properties of bread and how it changes when toasted.

Activities:
1. Each child has a slice of bread to describe.
2. They all toast their bread.
3. Each child describes their toast.
4. The three stages are recorded in their books as before.

The aims and activities can be seen to address, in various ways and at different levels, ability to:

1. Plan, hypothesise and predict.
2. Design and carry out investigations.
3. Interpret results and findings.
4. Draw inferences.
5. Communicate exploratory tasks and experiments.

These are fundamental skills of scientific exploration (Fagg and Skelton 1990).

Evaluation of the teaching activities and the children's responses

In general it was observed that all the children maintained interest and attention for the activities for the duration of the 50-minute lessons. Classroom management and organisation is an important aspect of differentiation which will influence children's ability to pay attention. In this case, they were not seriously distracted by other groups in the room except during Lesson 6 when the other children were whisking egg-white rather than making toast. This suggests that the decision to carry out the same activity as the other groups was practically beneficial. The willingness to participate and tendency to stay on topic rather than doing, or talking about, something else, was consistently maintained by the whole group. This was a particular achievement for three members of the group who did not always show such focus over a 50-minute period in other subjects.

The children's pictures and descriptions of what had happened were evidence that they developed their understanding of changes that occur in common events. The therapist's records of each lesson show that all children used the word *change* during the series of lessons and in the final assessment. They used the word in one or more of three contexts:

(a) Directly following an adult's model. For example,
    Therapist: Water changes flour.
    Child 2: Yes changes flour.
(b) When prompted by the adult the child used the sign for *change*.
(c) Spontaneously and unprompted. For example, during Lesson 5, Child 1 said 'chocolate change'.

Detailed records were kept of the progress and difficulties of each child. These are important in evaluating the teaching and they also contribute to the adult's understanding of the individual children's needs. Some of the information gathered has implications for teaching in other areas of the curriculum, for example the fact that some children make very obvious use of Paget Gorman signs in learning new words, or the severe difficulties with recalling a sequence demonstrated by Child 2. This information needs to be passed on to other adults involved with the children.

Each child's progress in relation to the learning objectives will now be considered in detail.

Child 1

This child participated enthusiastically in the practical activities but throughout the series of lessons she required prompting from the adult to record the process observed in a sequence of pictures. She could recall what had been done but not in the correct order. However, once she had drawn the pictures she was able to describe the stages to an adult using two- and three-word phrases.

From the first lesson she imitated the adult's use of the word *change* appropriately. In Lesson 4 she first used the word spontaneously. This child responded to prompting with the sign for *change* and also used the sign herself when saying the word in some situations.

Comparison of her two assessments shows that she used the word *change* when prompted (Figure 6.4).

Key concepts   **Child 1**

Concept question	Pre-topic date 9/96	Post-topic date 12/96
What happens when water gets very cold?	raining	no response
What happens if you take a lolly out in the sun?	off my coat	don't know
What happened to the Plasticine? (Changed shape)	it big it gone ball	1. gone (Adult cued PGSS sign for 'change') 2. change
What happened to the teddies? (Changed colour)	teddy teddy	1. blue – blue (Adult asked 'what did I do?') 2. change

Figure 6.4

Child 2

This child was the least confident about what the group was doing during the practical activities. He was able to take a turn by copying what another child had done but he was not able to make appropriate suggestions for what to do next. For example he thought the biscuits and icing could be eaten separately whereas the others had realised from the situation that the biscuits were to be iced first (Lesson 4).

Child 2 had severe difficulties recalling the activity in order to draw pictures. He was able to remember one or two actions but even when prompted he could not give appropriate responses for the other stages. The difficulty was confirmed when, having had help in drawing four pictures he was asked to describe the sequence. He was not able to do this in a meaningful way. For example in Lesson 2 he labelled his first picture 'breaking the jelly' and the second 'jelly in the packet'. This child was aware of his difficulty and responded well to the adult's attempts to help him. In Week 4 when he gave an appropriate response for the fourth picture in his sequence 'icing on biscuits' without the adult's help, he was very pleased with himself, recognising that he had said the right thing even before the therapist said anything and announcing with a relieved smile 'I'm right aren't I?'.

Child 2 used the word *change* spontaneously by Lesson 4. In his end-of-topic assessment he gave a much more complete response to the coloured bears item:

Child 2:   Yellow teddy bears gone.
Therapist: What did I do?
Child 2:   Changed them.

Key concepts	Child 2	

Concept question	Pre-topic date 9/96	Post-topic date 12/96
What happens when water gets very cold?	it will get cold it will drop	jelly
What happens if you take a lolly out in the sun?	it will melt	it melts
What happened to the Plasticine? (Changed shape)	it's like a doughnut	round shape
What happened to the teddies? (Changed colour)	yellow teddy bears	1. yellow teddy bears gone (Adult asked 'what did I do?') 2. changed them

Figure 6.5

Child 3

This child was frequently able to bring recall of previous experiences to the activities, making appropriate comments about what to do next when making jelly or crispie cakes. He was able to draw the sequence of pictures, regularly checking with an adult that he was correct or, if possible, copying another child. Despite this behaviour he was able to describe accurately what he had drawn and wrote three- or four-word phrases with help. Child 3 did not use the word *change* spontaneously but he did use it when prompted with the Paget Gorman sign both in lessons and in his final assessment.

When assessed (see Figure 6.6) he showed an improved understanding of the changes that occur in water.

Child 4

This child participated well in the activities. This was not a general feature of his behaviour in class, where he was often withdrawn and reluctant to join in. He was able to record in pictures and words what had been done, showing understanding that change had occurred.

He used the word *change* in imitation very quickly and by Lesson 4 he used it spontaneously.

In the post-topic assessment (see Figure 6.7) he needed a Paget Gorman sign to make any response to the Plasticine item. His response 'changing bread pink' to the bears changing colour was unfathomable.

It is known that this child does not take account of listener needs well, and therefore much of what he says depends on the listener being aware of previous incidents in his day.

Key concepts   **Child 3**

Concept question	Pre-topic date 9/96	Post-topic date 12/96
What happens when water gets very cold?	because it's very cold feeling cold	it's getting ice
What happens if you take a lolly out in the sun?	because it's getting sun	it's melted
What happened to the Plasticine? (Changed shape)	it's thunder it's getting stick	making a stick
What happened to the teddies? (Changed colour)	yellow	1. blue (Adult cued PGSS sign for 'change') 2. change

Figure 6.6

Key concepts   **Child 4**

Concept question	Pre-topic date 9/96	Post-topic date 12/96
What happens when water gets very cold?	snow	winter
What happens if you take a lolly out in the sun?	summertime ice cream	summer lick it
What happened to the Plasticine? (Changed shape)	it's raining and snowy thunder	(No response so adult signed 'change') 'change'
What happened to the teddies? (Changed colour)	yellow sun	changing bread pink

Figure 6.7

Child 5

As predicted, this child needed the help of the classroom assistant in order to maintain attention for the group activity and to take turns. With this help, she participated in all the lessons. She completed the work in her book, showing understanding of what had been done, except in Lesson 1 when she appeared to equate the meaning of 'change' with 'dissolve'. Therefore she said water did not change soil, flour, stone or sand but did change sugar and salt. Her responses therefore at this stage showed some element of accuracy but not complete understanding of the aims of the activity.

This child quickly used the word *change* spontaneously and also simultaneously used the Paget Gorman sign on several occasions.

Her assessment (Figure 6.8) shows that she had developed her understanding and expressive use of *change* during the term. She used the word spontaneously: 'change blue teddy bear'. She also showed that she now understood something about changes in water temperature:

Therapist: What happens when water gets very cold?
Child 5:   Ice.
Therapist: What happens if you take a lolly out in the sun?
Child 5:   Melt.

Key concepts   **Child 5**

Concept question	Pre-topic date 9/96	Post-topic date 12/96
What happens when water gets very cold?	raining	ice
What happens if you take a lolly out in the sun?	in the beach	melt
What happened to the Plasticine? (Changed shape)	oh longer sausages	squeeze playdough
What happened to the teddies? (Changed colour)	now blue teddy bears	change blue teddy bear

Figure 6.8

Evaluation of the therapist's work in the class

The teachers and therapist felt that there were advantages in organising small groups for science activities and always working with the same children. The arrangement gave continuity over the term. This was beneficial for the children since work could be approached in the same way each week and could be focused at an appropriate level and the adults could build on the experience of the previous lesson in very specific ways. The therapist was able to observe the progress of individual children and could give more time to the teaching of a few very simple aims than would have been possible in a larger group of more mixed ability.

Balanced against this however, the adults considered that there were two disadvantages. The children's class teacher did not directly experience the responses of these children to the science topic. She was able to hear the therapist's review and see the work in the children's books but she did not work on this topic at their level. Secondly, the therapist was only working with this group of children directly during the topic lessons. Although this was considered to be valuable because vocabulary, comprehension and interaction were all priorities addressed in topic work twice a week with the children, they all, additionally, had other, more individual and specific language targets for the year, which could not be addressed during these groups.

These difficulties could be overcome by changing the topic groups in the remaining two terms so that the therapist could take a different group in the class, allowing the teacher to work with the children at the lower language level. The therapist would then be able to use a different time in the week to work with these children on other aspects of language development. The decision for a speech and language therapist to work with groups in the curriculum does not mean that they will not also address children's individual needs at other times. Teachers and therapists will need to agree these practices together if maximum use is to be made of the time and of each other's skills and expertise.

Reflecting on the action

Reflection on the actions taken suggests that the experience of a speech and language therapist working in science lessons with one group of children could be justified for a number of reasons.

- The basic aims of the therapist's group were language-related. In the case of children with language and learning difficulties, it would be difficult to imagine planning curriculum activities without consideration of the language to be used and taught. Teacher and therapist collaboration would therefore always be a possibility.
- The classroom staff were willing for the therapist to take on this role and the therapist was willing to carry out the activities planned by the teacher. At the planning stages, therapist and teacher will have distinctive contributions to make from their particular experience and expertise. The teacher's contribution will be in curriculum and classroom management and the therapist's in language and communication analysis. However, at the stage of carrying out the plans, the two practitioners might be considered interchangeable.
- If there is concern that children are not 'receiving their fair share' or that other targets must be approached, rotation of groups can be arranged for the rest of the year to provide balance.

Reflection on the evaluation of each lesson and the children's progress suggests the following further steps.

- Child 2 requires further investigation of his recall skills and ways to develop these. Specific assessment may look at aspects of his memory and ability to process visual and auditory material to see whether there are particular areas of strength and weakness.
- Child 1 and Child 2 need work on ordering events in sequence and may benefit from specific activities to help these skills.
- Paget Gorman signs should be used systematically in the teaching of new vocabulary.

Curriculum issues

The experience and the information gained from these activities are evidence that children with very severe language impairment can benefit from science lessons in the classroom. The aims set must be appropriate and the amount of repetition needed must be allowed for. The fact that these children learn slowly and at a different level from their classmates must not become a reason for excluding them from areas of the curriculum.

Conclusion

There is a recurring argument in the school where this teaching took place that classroom work is of so little value to this group of children that they should have a mainly social education programme instead. While not denying the need to teach social skills, it is clear from the experience of these activities that these children can benefit from class-based activities when they are designed to meet their language needs. Indeed, it is possible to build social and interactional targets into other curriculum plans, such as the science lessons. By using the curriculum as a vehicle for language learning we can ensure that pupils will have access to learning opportunities similar to those of their peers while, at the same time, addressing their specific needs in the areas of language and communication.

Chapter 7

Differentiating Science

Introduction

From the earliest days of the National Curriculum in England and Wales, there was an implication that it was to be accessible to all pupils:

> All pupils share the same statutory entitlement to a broad and balanced curriculum, including access to the National Curriculum. (Department of Education and Science 1989, 8.1)

However, stating that pupils have an entitlement does not guarantee that they will receive it. Pupils with speech and language impairment frequently experience learning difficulties which make access to the curriculum an additional challenge to them and their teachers. Access to curriculum and to opportunities for demonstrating learning may be obscured by their difficulties with language and communication. Traditionally schools and teachers have used the spoken and written word to direct pupils' learning and to assess what they have learnt. Communication skills can be appropriately described as 'cross-curricular'. This has implications for both the language of instruction and methods of assessing pupils' knowledge, understanding and skills.

This chapter describes the teaching of a group of children in a special language unit. The evaluation suggests that the planning and management of their teaching and learning requires some considerations over and above those for some of their peers. With additional support the children can experience positive achievements.

In the primary school in which the teaching sessions took place a policy was in place which required each class teacher to produce a termly Forward Planning and Review Document, outlining proposed:

(i)   content
(ii)   time allocation
(iii)   method and organisation
(iv)   use of resources
(v)   relevant Attainment Targets of the National Curriculum

and a review and evaluation of the previous term's work.

In accordance with principles of curriculum entitlement, the policy included the teachers of the children with language difficulties, who were taught in a special unit in the school. National Curriculum circulars and guidance documents recommend the use of a cross-curricular approach to augment the basic curriculum and this approach had been adopted in the language unit. The teaching sessions which will be described and evaluated dealt with 'The Water Cycle' and were planned as part of a cross-curricular project on 'Water'. The project lasted one term and linked the Science, Maths, Technology, English and Geography elements of the National Curriculum. The sessions were planned and managed by the Unit teacher in consultation with a part-time speech and language therapist and the mainstream school's science coordinator. In order that pupils should be given the most appropriate opportunities to communicate their learning, Paget Gorman signing was used throughout the Unit to facilitate communication.

The children

The class comprised nine children, seven boys and two girls, aged between 8 and 11 years. These pupils experienced a variety of language and communication difficulties. (See Table 7.1.)

Table 7.1

	Age	School Year	Identified speech or language difficulty
Girl	11:06	6	Severe comprehension and expressive difficulties
Boy	10:09	5	Coordination difficulties (dyspraxia) with some language immaturities
Boy	10:06	5	Speech sound problems
Boy	10:05	5	Comprehension and expressive language difficulties
Boy	10:05	5	Dyspraxia, expressive language difficulties
Boy	9:01	4	Dyspraxia, expressive language difficulties
Boy	8:10	4	Dyspraxia, expressive language difficulties
Boy	8:07	3	Comprehension and expressive language delay
Girl	8:03	3	Semantic and pragmatic difficulties

Planning

As the first stage of planning, the staff prepared a content map of the curricular links across the theme of 'water' and how these were linked with National Curriculum Attainment Targets (see Figure 7.1).

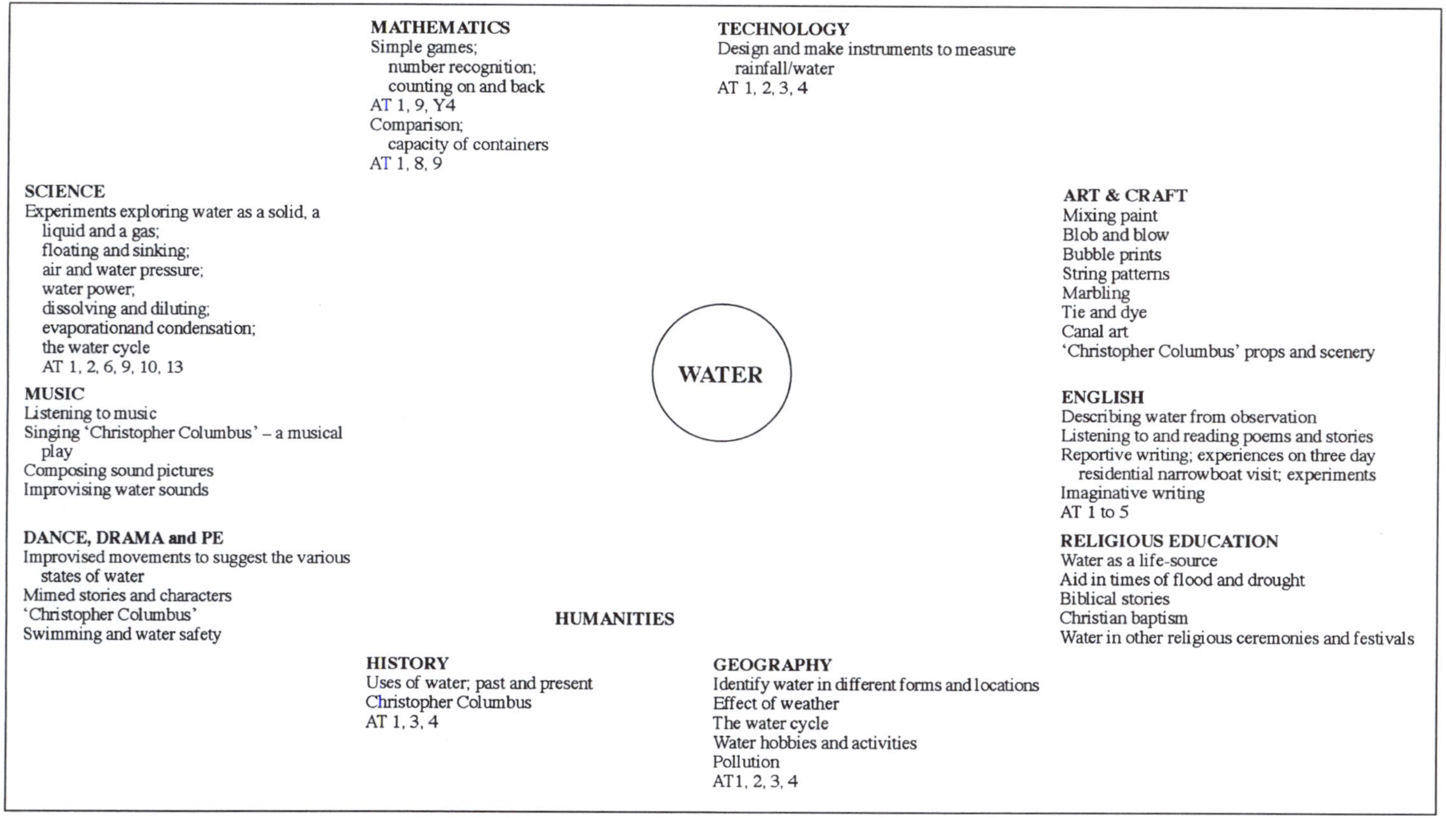

MATHEMATICS
Simple games;
number recognition;
counting on and back
AT 1, 9, Y4
Comparison;
capacity of containers
AT 1, 8, 9

TECHNOLOGY
Design and make instruments to measure
rainfall/water
AT 1, 2, 3, 4

ART & CRAFT
Mixing paint
Blob and blow
Bubble prints
String patterns
Marbling
Tie and dye
Canal art
'Christopher Columbus' props and scenery

ENGLISH
Describing water from observation
Listening to and reading poems and stories
Reportive writing; experiences on three day
residential narrowboat visit; experiments
Imaginative writing
AT 1 to 5

RELIGIOUS EDUCATION
Water as a life-source
Aid in times of flood and drought
Biblical stories
Christian baptism
Water in other religious ceremonies and festivals

SCIENCE
Experiments exploring water as a solid, a
liquid and a gas;
floating and sinking;
air and water pressure;
water power,
dissolving and diluting;
evaporation and condensation;
the water cycle
AT 1, 2, 6, 9, 10, 13

MUSIC
Listening to music
Singing 'Christopher Columbus' – a musical
play
Composing sound pictures
Improvising water sounds

DANCE, DRAMA and PE
Improvised movements to suggest the various
states of water
Mimed stories and characters
'Christopher Columbus'
Swimming and water safety

WATER

HUMANITIES

HISTORY
Uses of water; past and present
Christopher Columbus
AT 1, 3, 4

GEOGRAPHY
Identify water in different forms and locations
Effect of weather
The water cycle
Water hobbies and activities
Pollution
AT1, 2, 3, 4

Figure 7.1 Content map of 'water'

104

Science Attainment Target	National Curriculum Levels 1–5
AT 1	– observations
Exploration of	– asking 'how' and 'why' questions
Science	– formulating hypotheses
	– recording findings
AT 2	– to know that plants and animals need water to
The Variety of Life	sustain life
	– to sort living things into groups
AT 6	– exploring water as a solid, liquid and gas
Types and Uses of	– water power
Materials	– dissolving and diluting
AT 9	– water and weather
Earth and Atmosphere	– the water cycle
AT 10	– water pressure
Forces	– floating and sinking
	– water power
AT 13	– hot and cold
Energy	– water power
	– reservoirs, dams
	– water in the home

Figure 7.2 Forward Planning and Review Document Extract

The extract (Figure 7.2) from the Forward Planning and Review document shows how the proposed areas of study would link with National Curriculum targets in science.

The approach to planning was content-based but it was also important to plan for the development of concepts so that the children could be helped to understand broader ideas which would have more general use in their learning.

The basic concepts that this study was planned to cover were as follows:

1. Every living thing needs water.
2. More than half the world is covered by water.
3. Water moves from land to air and back to the land in a constant cycle.
4. Water can be a solid, a liquid or a gas.
5. Water can be useful: for example, for warmth, cleaning and energy.

6. Water can be dangerous.
7. Water can be fun.
8. Water can be beautiful.

An essential element of the planning process adopted by the staff in the language unit was time spent in attempting to assess the pupils' present knowledge and understanding of the subject matter and their likely interest in the subject. In this instance the whole group was involved in a brainstorming session to elicit responses to the question 'What do you know about water?'. Below are their responses:

Responses from four Year 5 boys
Water is some sort of liquid.
Things can float on water.
Fish can live in water.
Some mammals live in water.
Clouds have water in them.
Boats float on water.
Frogs live in water.
You can drink water.
Reservoirs contain water.

Water evaporates.
We can wash with water.
Water is H_2O.
Water goes through sewers.
People, animals and plants need water to live.
You can have fun in water.

Responses from two Year 4 boys and one Year 3 boy
Some people can swim in water.
Some people can float on water.
An island is surrounded by water.
Water turns icy when it gets cold.
Rain is water.
Some people sink in water.
Some water is salty.
Seals live in water.
Some birds live in water.

Responses from one Year 6 girl and one Year 3 girl
The sea is water.
Amy go swimming in water.
Amy drink orange and water.

This exercise indicated a high level of interest common to all the pupils but suggested considerable differences in their knowledge and understanding. The information gained from the activity would enable Unit staff to use each child's language as a guide to the level of language needed for them as individuals. The work of the speech and language therapist in the Unit was also incorporated into the curriculum and there was an attempt to take account of each child's individual therapy needs. It is important that therapy aims are, as far as possible, linked with children's everyday needs for language in the curriculum and therapists and teachers can profitably work together in this respect.

> For children with speech and language difficulties it is important to seize all opportunities presented in school, across the subject boundaries, where children are involved in talking, listening, questioning, reading and writing, as a means to help children actively uncover more about language itself. (Webster and McConnell 1987, p. 185)

In this way, many of the aims of speech and language therapy can be met in the classroom and the teacher's and therapist's knowledge and skills can be complementary.

Session 1

The content of the first session then, would be 'The Water Cycle' and would be based on the concept that water moves from land to air and back to land in a constant cycle. The intention was for the children to develop their skill in recording their observations. On this occasion the teacher would be alone as the speech therapist and the learning support assistant were unavailable.

Resources
The following resources were required

Saucer experiment set up three days earlier.
Portable cooker and pan.
Lemonade bottle with base removed to act as a bell jar.
Small container.
Video recorder and 'Watch' video (BBC 1988 – see information at end of References).
Worksheets, pencils, coloured pencils.
Books referring to the water cycle.

Group organisation

The session was planned to be in three parts. Part 1 would involve the whole group; in Part 2 the children would be divided into three groups, according to previously assessed knowledge and understanding; Part 3 would again involve the whole group.

Lesson Plan

The lesson was tightly scripted with clear reminders for the teacher about the language to be used.

Part 1: Introduction of topic
1. Examine rain gauge. Ask: Why is it empty?
2. Examine saucer. Ask: Where has the water gone?
3. Fill a small pan with water to a depth of 1 centimetre. Boil off the water until the pan is empty. Watch the steam rise. Ask: Where has the water gone?
4. Use lemonade bottle as a bell jar. Fill a small container with boiling water. Place bell jar over it. Watch steam fill the jar and condense into water droplets on the side of the jar.
5. Play 'Watch' video on water (15 minutes). Seek feedback from the children.

Total time for Part 1: approximately 45 minutes.

Part 2: Worksheets and assessment
Children to complete differentiated worksheets in three groups. Teacher to assess children's understanding of the water cycle by visiting each group in turn.
 Approximately 40 minutes for this part.

Part 3: Recap
Look at completed worksheets and recap on the sequence of events in the water cycle.
 Approximately 15 minutes for this part.

Evaluation

The introductory session promoted language and interaction. The children all seemed to understand that the rain gauges were empty because there had been no rain. They were initially surprised that the water in the saucer had disappeared.

On questioning, one child suggested that it had been tipped out. Most agreed that it had dried up. One boy suggested the heat from the sun was responsible. This method of teaching generally produces a high level of response and on this occasion the two experiments created considerable interest and generated plenty of spontaneous language. Although interesting and relevant in parts, the 'Watch' video contained information superfluous to the concept of the water cycle and was confusing for some children. The absence of support staff and the speech and language therapist meant that the confusion was not immediately apparent to the teacher. It was difficult to observe everything that was going on. The extracts in Figure 7.3 are from the Record and Assessment Sheets of three children. The sheets were designed by the Unit teacher along lines suggested in *The Primary Language Record* (Barrs *et al.* 1988). They are in daily use by all staff in the Unit.

Five of the children displayed a sound grasp of the concept; three showed reasonable understanding; one seemed very confused. One Year 5 boy compared the water cycle sequence of events to a 'story circle' told to the class during a creative writing workshop. At this pupil's suggestion all the children later made story hats depicting the water cycle. The confident way in which they approached this task indicated an understanding of the cyclical nature of the concept. It was less easy to assess their understanding of the actual processes involved. Each child had been asked the following questions:

Lakes, rivers and the sea are full of . . . ?
What does the sun do to the water in the lakes, rivers and the sea?
Where does the water go?
What happens to the water in the clouds when they get very heavy?

Some of the children were able to elaborate on the process. Some used words such as heat, energy and evaporation. Some were unable to answer more than one question appropriately.

This evaluation highlighted shortcomings in the initial planning process which had implications for future curriculum planning and teaching.

- A reduction in the usual staffing ratio for Science lessons from 3:9 to 1:9 appeared to have resulted in at least one of the children becoming confused and misunderstanding what was going on. Two of the more able children could possibly have been encouraged to pursue some lines of enquiry further had staff support been available.
- The 'Watch' video contained too much material for one session. It introduced ideas and information before some of the children were ready.
- Two worksheets were designed. Worksheet 1 was chosen to allow children to work at their own speed and to occupy them while the teacher gave attention to individuals. Worksheet 2 was designed for the more able pupils but was not sufficiently demanding for three of them.

SESSION 1

CHILD A

	TARGET	*ASSESSMENT*
Science Concept AT9 L5	Water Cycle – be able to explain the water cycle	Good understanding of cyclical nature of the process. Used 'evaporation', 'energy'. Water vapour was a new idea. Compare it with steam from kettle. Made suggestion re: story hats. R → M
Science Skill	(1) Complete Worksheets 1 and 2 without support (2) Respond appropriately to questions	(1) Too easy. Found actual text in book from class library. Copied. (2) 1√ 2√ 3√ 4√ Good use of vocabulary. M

CHILD B

Science Concept AT9 L2	Water Cycle – show understanding of the water cycle (weather)	Showed understanding in his oral description. 'Water goes round and round' Q. Is it always a liquid? A. No sometime it gas. R
Science Skill	(1) Complete Worksheets 1 and 2 with support (2) Respond appropriately to questions	(1) Careful colouring – much improved. Attempted Worksheet 2 on his own. Completed with help. (2) 1√ 2√ 3√ hesitated 4√ R

CHILD C

Science Concept AT9 L1	Water Cycle – be able to describe some stages in the water cycle (weather)	Confused by swimming pool sequence from 'Watch' video. I did not realise this until Part 2. She really was not sure what it had all been about. L
Science Skill	(1) Complete Worksheet 1 with support (2) Respond appropriately to questions	(1) Worksheet 1 seemed too much for her to take in. No real understanding of the representation. Arrow really confused her. (2) (1) children swimming (2) rain (3) don't know (4) break (after prompt) L

KEY: M – Mastered, R – Reasonable, L – Limited

Figure 7.3

110

- The questions devised to assess the children's understanding of the concept did not make enough provision for the different levels of ability.
- The session took place during a spell of dry weather. Whilst this was out of the teacher's control, it meant that there was no opportunity for the children to observe and experience the water cycle for themselves.

As a result of this evaluation and in consultation with the speech and language therapist, it was decided to 're-teach' the session and raise the topic again following a three-day residential visit aboard a narrow boat. During this time the children would be surrounded by water. It was also hoped that they would, by that time, have had the opportunity to observe the water cycle first hand. However, in the unlikely event of a continued drought, a video produced for Key Stage 1 pupils (age 5 to 7) was obtained, called 'Where does the rain go after it falls?' (Viewtech – see information at end of References). This video provided a starting point for the second session.

Session 2

The same content and concept were planned and again, children would use their skills of recording observations.

The teacher and support assistant would be available for the session.

Resources
The following resources were required:

Video recorder and video cassette
Worksheets 1, 2, 3 and 4 (see Figure 7.4), pencils, coloured pencils.
Tape recorder.

Group organisation
This time, the session would be in two parts. As before, Part 1 would involve the whole group and in Part 2 there would be three groups, one supported throughout by the support assistant.

Lesson Plan

Part 1
In the introduction, the whole group would be asked 'Where does the rain go after it falls?'. Children's responses would be recorded on the board. Watch video (9 minutes). Read through the worksheets in groups.

This part would take approximately 45 minutes.

Part 2: Worksheets
The teacher would assess children's understanding of the concept by individual questioning and response to worksheets.
   Approximately 45 minutes for this part.

Evaluation

The children made reference to their own experiences throughout this session. (It had rained for all or part of each day during the narrow boat visit.) Responses to the introductory question were recorded on the children's Record sheets. Two children did not offer responses in the introductory session but displayed an understanding of the responses made by others and gave appropriate responses themselves when questioned individually. Considerable time was spent reading through the worksheets prior to completion. The children appeared to know what they were looking for when they viewed the video for a second time. All three groups approached the task with enthusiasm. One pupil showed a good understanding of the concept but lacked the literacy skills to complete Worksheet 2 without help. He read the questions with the teacher and made his responses into a tape recorder. Some of the key words he used were written into his word book and he then completed the worksheet. The extracts (Figure 7.5) are taken from the Record and Assessment sheets of the same three children.
   The evaluation of the second session indicated an improvement in the five areas of concern. The children appeared to have been challenged at a more appropriate level and had been helped in their individual responses.

Worksheet 1

Watch the video again and then explain what happens in the water cycle. Draw pictures if it helps you to explain.

Figure 7.4 Session 2: Examples of worksheets used (continued)

Worksheet 2

Watch the video again and try to answer these questions.

1. When Wondercat looked around after the shower he noticed rain in many places.
   Can you remember three?
   Write them down.

2. We saw two creatures drinking water. What were they? Write down their names.

3. Wondercat saw rain water running down to a little stream. Where did it go next?

4. Where does most of the rain fall?

5. What happened to the rain water in the first puddle?

6. What happened to the water in the second puddle?

7. You can see liquid water. You can not see water vapour. True or false?

8. What makes the water and air warm?

9. Where do the droplets of water go?

10. When liquid water changes into water vapour it is called _____?

11. Water vapour collects into _____?

12. What happens when the clouds get black and heavy?

This is the water cycle.

Figure 7.4 Continued

Worksheet 3

Watch the video again. Read the word list. Fill in the missing words.

1. When rain falls some of it ———— into the ground.

2. Some makes ————.

3. Some goes into streams, rivers and ———— ————.

4. Water is warmed by the ———— and changes into water ————.

5. The water droplets join up to make ————.

6. Sometimes the clouds get black and heavy and they can not ————.

7. Then it ————.

8. The rain goes into the ————, ————, ————, ————, ———— and ————.

This is the water cycle.

Words you will need

clouds	float	ground
puddles	rains	rivers
the sea	sinks	streams
sun	vapour	

Work sheet 4

1st. The rain falls down.

2nd. The water goes into ————.

3rd. The sun dries up the water.

4th. The water goes up into clouds.

5th. The clouds get heavy and it rains.

This is the water cycle.

Figure 7.4 Continued

SESSION 2

CHILD A

	TARGET	*ASSESSMENT*
Science Concept AT9 L5	Water Cycle – be able to explain the water cycle	Explained accurately – referred to heat as energy from the sun, warm air rising, evaporation, water vapour as a gas. (Ask LSA to assess AT9 L5) M
Science Skill	Worksheet 1 – using reference books from class library	Less confident use of vocabulary in written work but included main points. R

CHILD B

Science Concept AT9 L2	Water Cycle – show understanding of the water cycle (weather)	Explained cycle, displayed good understanding of process and used 'weather' terminology with confidence. M
Science Skill	Worksheet 3 – using word list (unsupported)	Confident. Made reference to video and own experiences when questioned. Move onto frozen water, ice, snow. Water as a solid. M

CHILD C

Science Concept AT9 L1	Water Cycle – be able to identify 6 stages in the process using Worksheet 4 (ordinal number)	Worksheet gave cues. With support and signing she identified 6 stages. Assess without worksheet on Friday. R (Followed ordinal numbers correctly)
Science Skill	Worksheet 4 – complete unfinished pictures of 6 stages appropriately (supported)	Followed what her table did, had difficulty keeping in lines when colouring. Completing unfinished pictures proved perceptually difficult. L

KEY: M – Mastered, R – Reasonable, L – Limited

Figure 7.5

115

- The higher ratio of staff to pupils appeared to have helped the less able pupils to understand and to communicate their learning. In the first session the pupils were enthusiastic but some of them did not have the opportunity to express this enthusiasm to an adult. The group organisation in Session 1 did not promote initiation of language by the children. In the second session the presence of the additional adult made initiation a greater possibility.

- The video used during Session 2 was concerned only with the water cycle. It was shorter, kept the children's attention well and used vocabulary which was familiar to them. This suggests that greater care should be taken when selecting materials as teaching aids, particularly when introducing a concept which is new to some or all of the pupils.

- The worksheets used in the second session were produced by the teacher with specific children, aims and objectives in mind. They referred to experiences the children had had and observations they had made. They were designed to give them an opportunity to display an understanding of the water cycle at a level appropriate to their development. The teaching objectives for each pupil were the same, but the materials were modified to meet individual needs. Consequently, the outcomes were apparently more meaningful to the pupils and to the teachers during the second session.

- The questions used to assess the children's understanding gave greater consideration to the needs of individuals.

- When the second session took place the children had all observed at first hand: a river; clouds; rainfall; the effect of sun on puddles. Their responses to the question 'Where does rain go after it falls?' indicated that they had been able to draw on these observations when coming to terms with the concept that water moves from land to air and back to land in a constant cycle.

Conclusion

In the introduction to this chapter reference was made to pupils' entitlement to curriculum access. The role of the teacher is to facilitate this entitlement. The Forward Planning and Review document used in the school where the teaching took place encourages thoughtful planning and teaching of the National Curriculum. Record-keeping and assessment of individual children's knowledge, understanding and skills are an essential part of the planning process. However, during the course of teaching and re-teaching the two sessions it became apparent that more attention could be given to the review and evaluation of methods of teaching, staffing ratios, teaching aids and the presentation of tasks, particularly when questioning pupils for purposes of assessment. The planning and evaluation cycle must therefore include all aspects of children's and adults' activities in the process to inform judgements so that further refinement and differentiation can be achieved.

Chapter 8

Recording language in infants' Science lessons

Introduction

This chapter shows how detailed observation of the behaviour and language of individual children can lead to changes in practice and can enable the children to have opportunities more similar to their peers. In the sessions to be described, observation and evaluation of achievements were assisted by tape recording the sessions. National Curriculum documents remind us that children's questions and answers are strong indicators of their levels of achievement, their understanding and misunderstanding, the extent of their planning, the extent to which planned outcomes are being fulfilled, their attitudes to the activity and their changing levels of motivation (National Curriculum Council 1989a). These words can be daunting for those who have the responsibility of enabling access to the curriculum for children who have speech and language difficulties and for their assessment. The following science session and subsequent re-teach session took place with a group of 5 to 6 year olds who were at Year 1 in the National Curriculum.

The setting

The sessions took place in a mainstream infant and nursery school, catering for children aged between three and a half and seven. The year group had a high percentage of children from poor socio-economic backgrounds whose experiences and level of care, particularly health care, were limited. A large number of the children suffered from conductive hearing loss, resulting from frequent ear infections, which needed to be monitored carefully by health authority staff. Few children who entered the school had the necessary skills to direct their own learning. A school curriculum had therefore been developed which aimed to promote functional language and to present learning tasks in a structured way so that children could develop basic learning and organisational skills. The school day thus placed great emphasis on language development and social skills.

A unit for a maximum of twelve children with language and communication difficulties was an integral part of the mainstream school and nursery. The Unit provided children with the mainstream curriculum and the possibility of small group teaching and learning when necessary, with an emphasis on receptive and expressive language. Children accepted into the Unit had statements of special educational need or were at the final stage of assessment for a statement.

A full-time teacher was allocated to the Unit with, additionally, three part-time support teachers and one unit assistant for 24 hours per week. Two speech and language therapists also attended the Unit.

The sessions were carried out with a group of children from a year group of approximately 65 children. The year group was of mixed ability and had three children with identified speech and language difficulties with their peer group and one child with speech and language impairment who should have been in Year 2 but whose difficulties were so severe that a decision was made to retain him in his reception class for three terms. This was not considered ideal practice but staff believed that the opportunity to learn in the mainstream class was a better alternative than a 'special curriculum'.

The school had no science specialist but one member of staff undertook to coordinate this area.

Science in the infant curriculum

> The use of subjects to define the National Curriculum does not mean that teaching has to be organised and delivered within prescribed subject boundaries. (Department of Education and Science 1989)

Any subject presented in isolation is contrary to the integrated approach which is customary in primary schools and which is supported by the National Curriculum. Teaching very young children entails introducing material, giving experience, providing a variety of media for expression and reinforcement whenever the opportunity arises. In this school, each year group chose a half-termly topic appropriate to the age of the children. The topic for the content of this session was 'Change over time' and had been adopted as a whole-school topic. This topic was woven in to the whole curriculum and teachers drew up a topic web to provide a framework (Figure 8.1) .

Description of detailed planning

The topic web was created initially as a brainstorming activity. The year group class teachers, unit teacher, support teacher and speech and language therapist, worked through appropriate content and activities. Next an audit was carried out

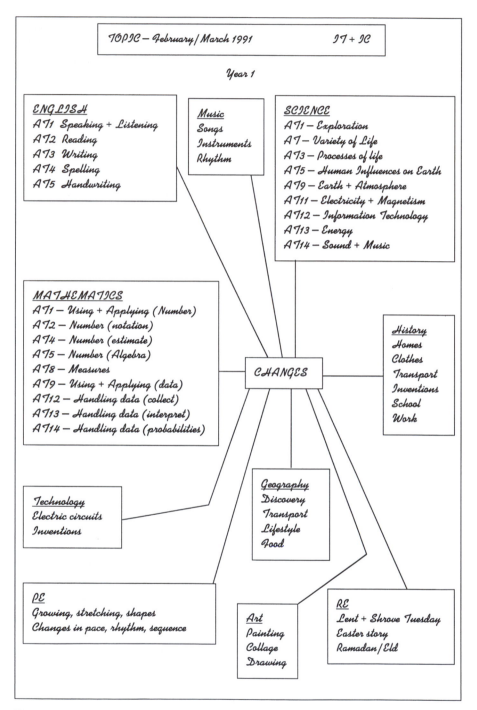

Figure 8.1

to ensure that all subject areas had been addressed, particularly the three core curriculum areas, maths, science and English. The team members then identified the relevant Attainment Targets. This is done in the knowledge that work in basic skills in maths and English is ongoing.

Traditionally, the infant curriculum covered much of the environmental science now identified in the National Curriculum. The child-centred pedagogy encouraged learning through a child's own experiences. However, the introduction of topics such as electricity and magnetism brought in aspects which many infant teachers felt ill-equipped to cope with. In order to acquaint themselves with the content of the Science component in the National Curriculum, the teachers in the school organised sessions to cover the components of their topic and also to follow up work in activity periods. At an evaluation meeting staff decided to continue this approach but identified specific skills and language needed to enable the children to progress across and through the science curriculum.

The children

Four children were of particular interest in these sessions. Each of them had language and communication difficulties which affected their learning skills and which required particular teaching strategies.

Gavin entered the school unable to speak and had his own signing system. He was strongly motivated to communicate, was beginning to verbalise and was rapidly acquiring new words. His difficulties with coordination (dyspraxia) were linked with problems of organisation and ordering of tasks and he had difficulties with both syllable order and word order. His need to concentrate hard on what he was going to say meant that he often did not attend to his speaking partner and he found turn-taking in conversation a great problem.

Matthew was sometimes able to use single and two-word phrases, but these were often unintelligible. He had difficulties finding the right word and would often continue to repeat (perseverate on) a word when he did find it. He was very aware of his verbal difficulties. He had good visual skills and could sequence patterns with beads and shapes.

Craig had limited intelligibility of speech. Perhaps because he was aware of his inadequacy in communication he often restricted his sentence length and changed what he had said when asked for clarification. He seemed to have a compulsive need to answer for everybody although this disappeared when he was with adults he did not know. He had good visual skills and his ability to listen was good, although he seemed to lack the ability to monitor his own speech and behaviour.

Shavar's speech production could appear normal to the casual listener. However, he had difficulty maintaining the topic of a conversation. He appeared to process speech very slowly and to take everything spoken literally. Subtle meanings and idiomatic phrases had to be explained to him. He often showed anxiety and preferred a calm quiet environment.

Organisation and planning

Unfortunately there were practical difficulties and some staff absences during this topic. The disruption to school organisation and routine was felt by all the children in the school and some of them reacted very badly to teachers they did not know. A supply support teacher was present during the session. She was allocated to the unit teacher and normal group arrangements were suspended. Usually, there were two class teachers, the unit teacher and support teacher, to work with 65 children. Staff had considered an integrated group system but had rejected this as support was not available throughout the whole day. Support therefore could not be guaranteed for children who had special educational needs, nor would it provide for adequate assessment on which to base future learning. Finally it was decided that a structured session would be followed by activities set out during the week. Further reinforcement of the learning could take place through story, poetry and movement. Art and craft activities, puzzles and an observation table would all be linked to the science content. The year band was usually divided into four groups which were not fixed and there was movement from group to group weekly. The children were allocated to a group depending on how much information they could understand at one time, the quality of concentration they could sustain and the level of their language. The science session was planned for a group of ten children, four of whom had speech and language impairment, two of whom had English as a second language, two had very irregular attendance and two had learning difficulties. These children were mixed in terms of cognitive skills but all had a specific need for support in language usage.

Flexibility of approach allows staff the freedom to help children with different levels of need. It is important to avoid over prescription in Programmes of Study in each foundation subject and to allow teachers to determine their own teaching approaches and ways of organising the programmes. The session was planned to form part of a whole experience, some structured and some integrated into class activities. The children in this group needed help to verbalise experience and observation. Indeed, they needed help to observe, they needed frequent revisits to topics in order that they could acquire relevant vocabulary and concepts; they needed help to organise and sustain concentration. The teacher responsible for this group of children had to strive to enable them to acquire the skills to make sense of what is going on around them. Collage stories, model making and drama, commonly used to promote learning in the infant classes, would make very little sense unless these children had basic understanding of the concepts involved.

Content planning

A meeting of the year team was held to plan the content of the science session. Throughout the year the children had worked on their own life cycle and it was decided to extend this to seeds, farm animals, frogs and butterflies. The team agreed that a colour mixing activity would make a good starting point. The children could mix colours and compare them with a colourful butterfly such as a tortoiseshell. This would lead on to detailed observation of a butterfly. The children would be invited to predict how a butterfly reproduced. The teacher would then present the life cycle and the children could record the cycle by sequencing a set of stages. The decision on how this would be undertaken and the materials to be used was left to the individual teachers but the unit teacher and speech and language therapist prepared a vocabulary list (Figure 8.2) so that all staff were aware of what children had to use and understand. The only real resources were some butterflies mounted in plastic discs.

It is important to see successful language learning in the early years as the outcome of collaboration between adults and children. Webster and McConnell (1987) suggest that when conditions for communication are right, the child's active impetus for language learning will be harnessed and the child will be motivated to discover language through using it. The adult facilitates interaction through language, responding to children's comments and questions and expanding on what they have to say. This approach places great emphasis on the child within an environment which the teacher must manage. The challenge for the teacher is to plan the dimensions of that environment and to implement the plan.

Language skills in the early years are closely linked with the child's learning in a whole range of contexts. The skills include: listening; naming; categorising;

Vocabulary list			
Nouns	**Verbs**	**Other**	**Concepts**
butterfly	drink	inside	life cycle
flower(s)	lay	on	hatching
nectar	hatch		variety of species
wing(s)			
feeler(s)			
eye(s)			
eggs			
leaves			
caterpillar			
skin			
chrysalis			

Figure 8.2

describing; denoting position; sequencing; reasoning. Several of these skills are relevant to understanding of science and this curriculum area is an ideal medium through which to develop language. The environment can be structured, there is activity and, in order to make sense of what is happening, there must be talk and listening.

Plan for Session 1

Objective: Exploration of Science (Attainment Target 1)

1. To give children opportunity to mix primary colours and observe results.
2. To compare colours achieved with colours on picture of tortoiseshell butterfly.
3. To observe butterflies through a hand lens.

Activity: colour mixing.

Discussion: – individual – colours obtained
                 – group – tortoiseshell butterfly.

Observation: butterflies with a hand lens.

Resources
paint
brushes
palettes
water
paper
picture
hand lenses
mounted butterflies

Working area: dining hall (we must leave by 11.40 a.m.)

Staff: Ask speech and language therapist to observe and take part in discussion; request help in assessing vocabulary known.
No support.
In groups – teacher-directed pairs.
E2L children – repeat and rephrase.

Focus on
Matthew, Craig – encourage verbalisation.

124

Gavin – insist on turn-taking and listening to others.
Shavar – comprehension; ask questions.
Ryan – monitor contextual language.
Gursimran – ensure that he participates in the activity.

Objectives to be taken into account

Gavin
Firmly insist that he takes his turn in speaking.
Demonstrate the need to listen to others by pointing out something he has missed.
Model acceptable sequence of words in a sentence.
Remind him to look at a speaker.
Encourage retelling of events.

Matthew
Allow time for a verbal response.
Invite any verbal response.
Promote asking 'what' questions as this is a target in therapy. Hold something out but offer no explanation.

Craig
Encourage use of 'I didn't say that' when partner mishears.
Monitor responses; listen for word endings such as plurals and -ed on past tense.
Discourage interruption by saying 'It's not your turn'.
Target him for answer or contribution – he can be missed out as speech is hard work.

Shavar
Rephrase and reassure when he looks worried.
Encourage close observation and prediction.
Try to pursue his misunderstandings.
Ask true/false questions and nonsense questions.

The session

Since the regular support teacher was absent the groups were revised and on this occasion there were 15 children. The supply teacher agreed to take the discussion session so that the unit teacher could observe. The discussion was taped and transcribed. The children were paired at the direction of the teacher and asked to choose by name two primary colours for mixing. They were asked to make this decision jointly but they found this very difficult and were confused by being asked to work as a pair with just one piece of paper. Eventually they were all mixing and managing to label the colours they had made. One child asked to use the colours to make a pattern. Soon all the children were making patterns and followed the lead of this child who was now folding his paper and spreading the paint. He was heard to cry 'Hey I've got a butterfly' and all of the children in the group attempted to make a butterfly shape. Colour mixing was now forgotten but the outcome for the children was heading in the right direction. This had taken most of the morning session.

The discussion session was led by the supply teacher whom the children did not know and who did not know the children. The group also had to find a new location as the dining hall was required by dinner staff. This move unsettled the children. However most of them showed interest in the pictures they were talking about and they were very excited when given the plastic hand lenses. Although the children had used magnifying glasses before, they had never encountered the rectangular plastic ones without a handle which had been selected for this session. They had great difficulty in using them to see the butterflies and the two teachers decided to allow the children to look at various parts of their own and their partner's bodies so they could practise using the lenses. The session ended and the planned content had not been covered.

Evaluation

The children had no concrete outcome from the session except their painted butterflies which adorned their classrooms. The unit teacher made observation notes for each child on a sheet which was added to each day. She recorded that Gavin, Matthew, Craig and Shavar had all done colour mixing but they had found difficulty working on a joint task. They had all been able to label accurately the colours they had used and created. She noted that observation of butterflies with the hand lenses had not been covered adequately. The group discussion had also been tape recorded and this, together with the observation, was useful in revealing many features which could be changed for the next session. Taping and transcribing are very lengthy processes but can isolate important points which can easily be missed at the time. The following were noted:

- The pictures to be discussed were too complex.
- The children had chosen where to sit and most were seated so that they could not see one anothers' faces.
- Gavin rose seven times and made to strike another child. He took up much teacher time. He also frequently took other children's speaking time.
- Craig and some of the other children did not speak throughout the entire session.

- The teacher missed the opportunity to lead the children on to the life cycle.
- The tape revealed that the teacher used many conditional sentences, for example:

    'Good boy, I think *it might be* a butterfly'

    'Ryan, are you listening because *I might choose you*'.

    It was possible that this particular grammatical structure was difficult for some children to understand.

- Shavar seemed to experience particular difficulty and looked very worried and confused throughout. The following extract from the transcription shows an example of an exchange which probably contributed to his confusion.

Speaker	Line	Transcription	Comment
Teacher	160	what did she say she could see Shavar?	
S	161	(sled)	
D	162	stalk	
T	163	no she said eyes at first but she said something	
T	164	else Shavar	
S	165	er	
T	166	tell him again Amika	
A	167	leaf	A and S lost topic

Discussion changes topic here and children and teacher discuss dandelions and return to butterflies near the end of the session.

The observation suggested that the four children with speech and language difficulties had acquired most of the vocabulary. In Matthew's case he could attempt most of the words and could point out the words he could not say.

Vocabulary	Craig	Gavin	Matthew	Shavar
butterfly	√	√	√	√
egg	√	√	√	√
insect	-	-	-	-
fly	√	√	√	√
caterpillar	√	√	√	√
chrysalis	√	-	√	-
body	√	-	√	√
feelers	√	√	√	√
wings	√	√	√	√
eyes	√	√	√	√

The children had not however, observed and commented upon a butterfly and at the next planning meeting of the year group it was obviousthat the other groups had covered much more ground.

Session 2 Planning

Session 2 was planned as a revisit and further development of the same topic using information from the observations of individual children and the reports from the other groups. Class teachers agreed that they would try to do the life cycle for their children using a children's book on butterflies. The worksheet used by the other groups would be adapted and group cooperation would be encouraged rather than working in pairs. (Copies of the original and adapted worksheets are shown as Figures 8.3 and 8.4 at the end of this chapter, pp. 133/4.)

Objective: Processes of life

1. To give each child the opportunity to observe with a hand lens.
2. To comment as a group on what was observed.
3. To discuss the life cycle of a butterfly.
4. To sequence stages of the life cycle.

Activity: – Drawing a butterfly;
– Cutting up and sequencing four stages of the cycle (differentiated).

Discussion: of observations and pictures. (Circle arrangement for seating.)

Observation: butterflies with a hand lens.

Resources
black felt pens
paper
mounted butterflies
hand lenses with handle – some on stands if possible
scissors
glue

Working area: Unit resources room. No helpers.

Staff: Teacher only.
E2L children – rephrase often.

Focus on

Matthew – give much encouragement; he is showing great interest.

Gavin – expect better listening behaviour; encourage reasonable questions.

Ryan – be aware when he looks anxious and 'ease up'.

Craig – give him time to verbalise as he missed out last week.

Shavar – watch out for misunderstanding – pursue and clarify if possible.

Gursimran – give help with activity.

The session

For Session 2 there were only ten children in the group. They were seated in a circle with the teacher as a member of the circle, this enabled the children to see everyone who spoke. They were invited to comment in turn on what they could see, with a rule that they must speak only when it was their turn.

They were given magnifying glasses with a handle and asked to draw what they could see and to use only a black pen in order not to distract them from the detail. Individually children were asked to comment on their pictures and to give their version of how a butterfly has its babies. They were then asked to cut up the adapted worksheet and stick the picture in a book so that they told the story.

Evaluation

The transcription was used extensively to ascertain changes in the children's behaviour and understanding. It could be seen that all of the children had improved in turn-taking. Additionally, all of the children from the language unit could now either name or point to specific details on a butterfly. They demonstrated from what they said that they had a developing knowledge of the life cycle of a butterfly. The transcription suggests that Gavin was now thinking about the lifestyle of a butterfly.

Speaker	*Line*	*Transcription*	*Comment*
Teacher	67	and in	
T	68	the flower there is some lovely sugary water	
T	69	called nectar	
G	70	nectar	
T	71	and that's what the butterfly drinks no solid	
T	72	food	
G	73	no dead food	

Shavar was following the conversation sufficiently to correct a slip made by the teacher:

Teacher	100	the butterfly drinks flower from the nectar
Shavar	101	nectar from the flower
Teacher	102	nectar from the flower

He was also able to predict, although not accurately, what a butterfly might eat – 'rice'.

Matthew needed much praise and teacher time but the transcription shows that he follows the cycle and can offer single words appropriately when the unit teacher offers the opportunity to fill in the missing gap.

Teacher	155	and out comes not a caterpillar	
	156	remember there was a caterpillar in there	
	157	out comes	
Matthew	158	butterfly	(very clear)

Matthew responds correctly and clearly with 'butterfly'.

Matthew had shown particular interest in the session. His understanding of science had been difficult to assess because he offered no response and he had in the past distracted other children. These lessons proved to be a turning point for him and he began to bring books from home to point out animals.

Unfortunately Craig had missed this session but in an individual conversation with the teacher it was clear that he could retell the life cycle but time was needed to decode his almost-unintelligible speech.

The transcription of Gavin's conversation with the teacher showed that he had asked some pertinent questions rather than chipping in.

Speaker	Line	Transcription	Comment
G	1	They spin	
T	2	They do spin a bit like spiders they spin a	
T	3	thread	
G	4	Why spin a web	
T	5	They don't spin a web what they do is spin	
T	6	right around themselves to make a chrysalis	
T	7	and they leave one or two threads and fasten	
T	8	the chrysalis on to something. That's very clever	
G	9	a butterfly a why a why er fly away em	
T	10	what do you mean	
G	11	why a why fly away	
T	12	when do you mean when do you mean	

G	13	no [pause] why
T	14	why do you mean when it's hatched out
G	15	yea
T	16	it needs to feed doesn't it

Ryan and Gursimran were not clear about the cycle but could identify details with help and they did attempt a picture. All children managed to sequence their pictures but then sticking them on to paper caused them to confuse the correct sequence. Gursimran and Ryan had needed individual help here.

The unit teacher recorded these points on the observation sheets for each child. The second session had been heavily structured by the teacher but the children had given more evidence that they had reached the objective. In the cases of Gursimran and Ryan it had become clear that they had not, but that they had experienced and gained something at their level.

Further developments

An observation which needed particular consideration was the confusion which arose when a correct sequence of pictures had to be transferred to a book. The teacher thought that next time, numbering these pictures could be helpful to the children and that instead of a book with pages the children could be offered a linear book which could be folded at the end of production.

Some children had responded to the pictures in the butterfly book but as each page must be viewed in isolation the children may not have understood the sequential nature of the information. A zigzag, concertina-style book was found which allowed the teacher to build a sequence (Rylands 1974). This book has no text and allows children to tell their own story. Some easy-to-make puppets on sticks were also suggested which allow children, either on their own or with other children, to recreate the story. These could easily be adapted for other animals and events and would allow the children to be involved in developing their own sequence, making the event more real perhaps than looking at pictures. There was also the possibility of finding real butterflies if an outdoor lesson could be arranged.

The difficulty in finding resources to meet the needs of children with particular difficulties in language processing was a challenge to the teacher and as a consequence the unit teacher developed an information pack for supply teachers. The pack explained some of the problems experienced by children with speech and language difficulties and suggested how materials could be organised.

One of the disadvantages of planning lessons in such detail can be that teachers may be afraid to divert from the plan as so much organisation is required to teach and then assess learning that has taken place. In the infant curriculum, it is also important to maximise use of spontaneous opportunites which arise. The team agreed that an opportunity to see a real butterfly out of doors would have provided a valuable complementary session. Ways must be found of recording children's responses to spontaneously occurring day-to-day activities and of linking these with more formal teaching targets.

Although transcription is a time-consuming and skilled activity, its value can be enormous in focusing attention on the exact nature of teachers' and children's language. It is not suggested that recording and transcription of every session should be undertaken but that from time to time it can be used to provide concrete evidence of children's understanding and achievements. It is also valuable in raising adults' awareness of their spoken language and how it is matched with the children's learning.

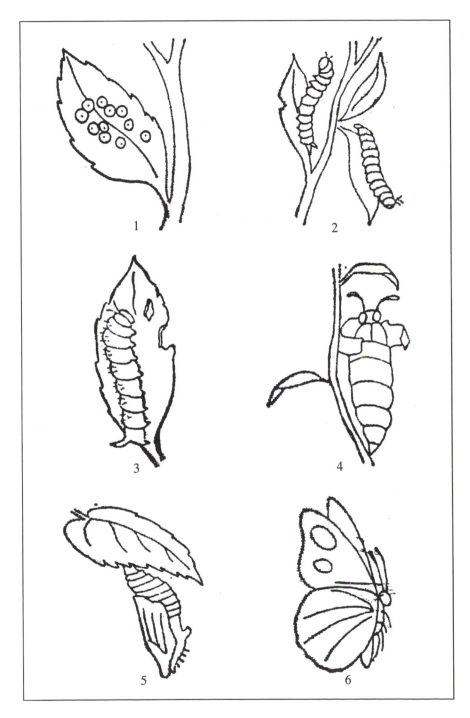

Figure 8.3 Worksheet used by other groups.

Figure 8.4 Adapted worksheet

Chapter 9

Music for children with severe learning difficulties

Introduction

The importance of language and communication can be demonstrated in all aspects of teaching and learning and, in recent years, with the introduction of new curriculum guidelines across the UK, schools have increased the emphasis on speaking and listening. The focus in this chapter is a group of children in a special school, where the teacher and the speech and language therapist had discussed the importance of raising the profile of language and vocabulary in a more specific way in all subjects. In this case, music lessons provide the context for a range of language and communication targets. The chapter also demonstrates how communication between staff was improved by developing better planning and recording sheets which were accessible to all of the practitioners involved.

The children

The children were aged 7 to 10 years and experienced a variety of learning difficulties linked with general developmental difficulties. These were seen as difficulties with attention, memory and comprehension, as well as difficulties associated with physical disabilities. All of the children had language and communication difficulties and one child, Michael (MG), had little means of expression.

Planning and rationale

The class was involved in a topic theme of 'Myself and my Family' for the duration of this project which ran over seven sessions. It was normal practice to link the music with the class topic.

The children had a music lesson once a week, the class generally working as a whole group with opportunities for individual and paired work. Although taught in a group, it was essential that the teacher also planned for individual needs in lessons. All pupils therefore had individual targets which were reflected in the planning and organisation of each lesson and were assessed and reviewed termly. Differentiation was by outcome for most of the pupils. This means that the aim of each lesson was different for each of them, even though they all participated in similar activities. The main exception to this was Michael, whose particular learning difficulties could prevent him from working as part of a group for the whole of the lesson. This pupil's work had a range of alternative activities built in, enabling him to remain in the room and to be part of the group wherever possible. The introduction of symbol cards to help him to express choices proved to be very useful as he had almost no intelligible speech. Following discussion with the class teacher and the speech and language therapist, by the end of the term Michael was using a symbols board for music and to indicate needs in his classroom. This increased his expressive ability and his parents were also being encouraged to use a communication board at home.

The planning

The content of the music lessons was derived from the Derbyshire Advisory Schedule (Derbyshire Advisory and Inspection Service 1995) and the Programmes of Study from National Curriculum Key Stage 1 Music, as these were more appropriate to the pupils' abilities than Key Stage 2. The areas included listening to recorded music, singing, using instruments, composing and an introduction to symbolic notation. (See Table 9.1.)

There was an additional element of including some aspect of written language to meet the requirements of this study module. However, although the planning of the music lesson would be for the whole group, the additional written element would be for two pupils only as it was unrealistic to expect other pupils in the group to achieve this.

A vocabulary list to be used in the planning of the music lessons was drawn up. This included both vocabulary of the current class topic, for example, names of people; names of body parts and vocabulary linked with music, in this instance, 'loud' and 'quiet'. Development of the children's functional communication was an important aim and speaking, singing and signing were all to be encouraged. The lessons were thus planned to meet the National Curriculum requirements and also to address the needs of pupils with severe learning difficulties.

The teacher had previously planned lessons in a written format, which, although not difficult to understand, could not be consulted quickly by other staff or act as a teaching prompt during the lesson. The first task therefore, was to devise a pro forma which would incorporate the required planning elements in a

Table 9.1 Individual targets: September 1996

Target	National curriculum programme of study	Pupil
1. To sing a chorus of a song, supported by sign or gesture alongside other pupils	KS1 5a	SG, SP
2. To respond to graphic signs for loud and quiet sounds, using both voice and instruments	KS1 5b	SG, RM SP, PH
3. To clap a 3 pulse rhythm in a regular beat	KS1 5a	RM
4. To clap a 4 pulse rhythm in a regular beat	KS1 5a	PH, SP
5. To use a shaker to shake when music is played	KS1 1a	RC
6. To indicate a preference for a musical activity from a given choice	KS1 1a	RC
7. To choose either a Walkman or a drum from a symbol	KS1 6d	MG
8. To tap a tambour quietly or loudly with verbal prompts	KS1 2c	MG

clear and precise way which could be understood by all staff involved. The pro forma for the scheme of work (Figure 9.1) was developed which provided a format for planning each lesson. The pro forma ensured that all the elements of aims, individual targets, resources and National Curriculum requirements were addressed on a single sheet of paper for each lesson. Staff roles and reponsibilities in the lessons could be easily identified and the activities for each child could be checked.

Lesson 1 was planned (Figure 9.2) to incorporate a range of activities which could be expected to capture and maintain the children's attention over short periods. A variety of music would be introduced to enable the children to experience 'loud' and 'quiet'. Songs and chants using body vocabulary and children's names would be used. Symbol cards with smiling and sad faces would be used to represent 'sad' and 'happy'. These were planned to help the children to understand and indicate 'sad' and 'happy' so that they could attempt to evaluate their own reactions to the activities. The teacher had the support of two learning

SCHEME OF WORK FOR MUSIC		TOPIC – MYSELF	DATE – SEPTEMBER	
NATIONAL CURRICULUM PROGRAMME OF STUDY	AIMS	INDIVIDUAL TARGETS	PUPIL'S INITIALS	RESOURCES
1. KS1 – 2c, 6b, d	To be able to recognise loud and quiet music	1. To clap a 3-pulse rhythm in a regular beat	RM	Instruments
2. KS1 – 5a	To clap rhythms to words which name body parts	2. To clap a 4-pulse rhythm in a regular beat	PH, SP, SG	Symbols cards for sad and happy
3. KS1 – 5b	To respond vocally to symbols for happy and sad as a chant	3. To sing/sign a song as part of a group	PH, SP, SG, RM	Pictures for sad and happy
4. KS1 – 5c	To sing/sign 2 new songs	4. To shake a shaker when music is played	RC	Tape recorder
5. KS1 – 4a	To experiment with untuned percussion + tuned notes which contrast high and low	5. To use a Walkman to listen to music for a few minutes at a time	MG	Songs – One big family
6. KS1 – 1b, 4f	To record some work on tape and for pupils to evaluate it	6. To tap an instrument loudly and quietly with verbal prompts	MG	Clap your hands Classical music to contrast loud and quiet
English – KS1 – S & L – 1d, 2b, 3b		7. To chant in response to a symbol	PH, SG, SP, RM	Pupil evaluation sheets
Writing – 1b, 2b		8. To express a preference for a musical activity	PPH, SPP, SG, RC, MG	STAFF
				JG – teacher PB – ECO GT – ECO

	TIME
LANGUAGE	7 lessons – 45 minutes each
Vocabulary names, family names, body parts, colours loud/quiet, sad/happy	
Expression express a preference/give opinion, discuss self-evaluation, comment on mood of music, recall	
Writing copy-write sentence (2 pupils)	

Figure 9.1

LESSON 1 MUSIC	20 September	45 minutes

AIMS
1. To introduce the concept of quiet music
2. For pupils to use sad/happy face cards – with chant – sad – low pitch, happy – high pitch, using voices only
3. To use clapping rhythm for parts of the body
4. To introduce to new songs and to practise singing the choruses of each
5. For pupils to express a preference for the part of the lesson they liked best

RESOURCES
Music – Cavatina, song tapes, Calypso tape
Instruments – range of percussion, chime bars
Walkman and tambour for MG
Sad/happy picture cards

CONTENT
1. Cavatina – music on arrival *Discuss loudness, quietness – ask for pupil ideas*
2. Naming song for each child – Hello, Peter, etc. Begin very quietly, then increase volume. *Ask for pupil observations*
3. Introduce percussion instruments. *Pupils to decide which are loud and which quiet.* Use to tap a beat while singing 'Hello' song
4. Identify body parts with 1 to 4 syllable words. *Feet, toes, blue eyes, quiet hands, noisy lips, two round knees arms that reach high.* Clap rhythms singly, then build up
   Pupils could choose 1 to clap alone (evaluate). Chant 'sad, sad', etc. while pointing to each card
5. Use sad side face cards, lined up. Chant 'sad, sad'. etc. while pointing to each card
   Use activity pictures. *Pupils to state preference for 'happy' activity*
   Change sad face to happy one. Repeat chant. Continue until everyone has had a turn.
   Use high and low tone chime bar to reinforce difference. Staff to demonstrate
6. Song – One big family. Listen first, repeat chorus with signs and words
7. Song – Clap your hands – as above
8. *Use picture prompts to discuss which parts of the lesson pupils likes best*
9. West Indian-style music to dance to for the end of lesson
10. SP and SG to talk about music and to draw and cop-write

CONTEXT   **INDIVIDUAL**
MG – to be part of the group for activities 1 and 2
RC – to choose instrument
MG – can choose Walkman music if he wishes
RM – work particularly on 1 and 2 beat names
SG, PH, SP – to try rhythm with chime bars
SG – to be encouraged to sing and sign all key words
MG – to have tambour and play quietly
Other pupils to return to class

Figure 9.2

139

INDIVIDUAL EVALUATION

NAME	SG	SUBJECT	Music
DATE	COMMENTS – ACTIVITY	LANGUAGE	
20.9	Chose instrument to play but did not play it	Individual prompting to join song	
27.9	More active – played wooden instrument at appropriate time	3-word sentence 'He bang there' Joined in some words of a familiar song	
4.10	Enthusiastic work on chime bars	Also got up and danced for first time today	
11.10	Joined 'Happy' song with clapping action Absent	Joined ostinato rhythms verbally, could not tap at same time	
18.10	Dancing to opening music, copying H but actions appropriate Responded correctly to noise symbols and conducted	Used voice for body chant, joined some words of choruses 3-word expression noted, no evidence of 2-syllable words	
25.10	Copying PH – but not positive today. Poor concentration	Sang most of body chant today with PH Most words articulated in correct order	
8.11	Absent Need to complete evaluation when SG returns to school	Commented with single words to music 'like', 'noise'	

Figure 9.3

support assistants during each lesson (known in the school as Educational Care Officers – ECO). They were involved in the initial planning and were given notes prior to each lesson. The assistants joined in the lessons as models for the children and participants alongside the teacher. Additionally, they took turns to work alongside Michael, who needed a person with him at all times.

A range of resources was chosen to provide opportunities for the pupils to express and develop their musical skills through listening, looking, moving and singing. They included instruments, pictures, symbols, recorded music and songs.

Recording

The nature of the children's difficulties suggested that it was essential to maintain a record of very small achievements. The teacher developed a simple format to record individual performance each week. This noted activities and any indications of understanding or expressive language. (See example of the completed form for child SG, Figure 9.3.) These records provided an important source of information for writing the pupils' annual reports.

Each lesson was evaluated as soon as possible afterwards otherwise it was very easy to forget some detail and small steps of progress observed. The information was then used to inform the next lesson's planning.

Observations on Lesson 1

- In the first two activities, pupils did not recognise the music as being 'quiet', although they all sat very quietly and listened for several minutes. On reflection, it appeared that they associated 'quiet' with no noise at all and therefore even quiet music might still be classed as a 'noise'. Larger differences between stimuli are often needed for these children because of their learning difficulties. It might be better in the first instance to use the greater contrast between silence and music as a step to helping the children to understand this concept.
- The pupils did recognise loud and quiet when using their voices in the 'Hello' songs. Instruments were added but their noise level was not discussed. This would be done next time.
- Pupils enjoyed clapping as a group and naming body parts as a sequence. Individual performances were not asked for. These would be checked in the next lesson.
- Pupils focused well on the 'face' cards and understood the chant sequence. Sam (SP) 'conducted' the group by pointing to the cards in order. He then played the rhythms on the glockenspiel. Others also tried this.

141

- The children were enthusiastic about the taped songs and it was decided to repeat this in the next lesson.
- The teacher talked about their response to different parts of the lesson with picture prompts. This was the first time they had been used. Most pupils said they 'liked' everything; this was noted as an area for future work which would help the children to become more aware of themselves and of their own reactions and feelings.

Comments on individual pupils

Polly (PH): coordinated spontaneous dance movements to the opening music.

Richard (RC): answered correctly a question asked of the whole group 'Whose name made a quiet sound?' Chose bells and shook them spasmodically at appropriate times.

Michael (MG): used Walkman for a few minutes, twice. Tried, with physical prompts to tap a tambour quietly at the end of the lesson.

Steve (SG): joined in songs only when individually prompted. Chose instrument but did not really experiment with the sounds.

Ruth (RM): joined in parts of songs. Attempted clapping rhythms for two-word sequences.

Sam (SP): played subdued and lively rhythms for 'sad' and 'happy' faces on several occasions. Joined in the chant and understood what was required.

Subsequent sessions

In the following sessions, the teacher kept individual records. Extracts indicate changes in children's responses.

Lesson 2
A new pupil had joined the class the previous day. DK had been out of a school environment for some months and his behaviour was very challenging. He was in a wheelchair which he could control and this caused disruption to the lesson after the first ten minutes.

Initial activity with musical contrasts was quite effective. Most pupils began to recognise the difference between loud and quiet in this context.

In 'Hello' song PH began to introduce other pupils and staff. Other pupils began to take the initiative for whether their name was to be loud or quiet.

Lesson 3
Generally much better this week. DK was now part of the group and cooperated for most of the session.

Due to the similarity between the activities of this week and last week the pupils were becoming familiar with the format and what was expected. Improved performance was noted for most of the pupils.

The section in which the repeated (ostinato) rhythms were played with voices and instruments was particularly successful, pupils responded to the loud and quiet voices being used without being told what to do.

Lesson 4
Good response to different music this week: March of the Hebrew Slaves, followed by Jesu Joy of Man's Desiring. Pupils visibly calm and quiet during second piece. PH responded with dance to both. Pupils chose the second piece to listen to again at the end of the lesson.

Ostinato rhythms were not as successful vocally this week, but pupils did develop rhythms just using chime bars and glockenspiels and continued with a sensitive reaction to each other playing loudly or quietly and fading to a natural end. Introduce symbols for loud and quiet next week and use initially for voices only.

Enthusiastic singing at the end of the lesson. Class teacher had used tape during the week to reinforce words and music. DK requested another song to sing.

Put coloured sticker on Walkman to identify play button for MG. If he cannot manage this, use a larger switch mechanism to give him more independence.

Lesson 5
Showed some appropriate responses to music – slow movements and much livelier positive movements. When 'Hebrew Slaves' was repeated at the end of the lesson, several pupils picked up instruments and played along with the strong beat.

Pupils becoming more aware of how to use the instruments appropriately; responded to loud and quiet symbol cards. Used these while playing rather than singing as in the orginal plan.

Pupils were so keen to dance to songs this week that very little singing was achieved to the two usual songs. However sang an old favourite to finish and they sang and signed to this one.

Lesson 6
Three pupils were absent (RC, SP, DK) so the group structure was different. This seemed to affect pupils' responses in some parts.

PH, RM, SG all identified the difference between the loud and quiet music. It was interesting to note that they were now able to do this even though this week one of the pieces used voices and not just instruments.

'Hello' song – all participated including MG. PH tried to direct others to choose loud or quiet singing – 'Loud, she want it loud'.

Name rhythms – RM was able to identify her own and attempted to clap. PH and SG could not identify their own but did clap them correctly when shown.

MG – unable to settle to any activity, wanting to bang loudly on drum, disliked music on Walkman and threw it. This then began to affect the others, particularly PH's behaviour.

Attempted to use symbol cards for loud and quiet, using glockenspiels and xylophones. PH enjoyed conducting when it was his turn, but was less enthusiastic about playing today. Taped the music and it was clear to the pupils which were the loud and quiet parts. They identified them by pointing to the appropriate symbol.

General behaviour of all the pupils today was more unpredictable than normal.

Pupils Steve and Sam
Two pupils, Steve (SG) and Sam (SP) were to have undertaken a written element. The original intention was for these two pupils, after the first lesson, to discuss and write about what they had done. However, as the lesson immediately following this was drama, a favourite activity on Friday afternoons, both pupils were very reluctant to stay. In considering their lesson for the next week, the teacher decided to see these pupils on the Monday, following the second music lesson. The lesson was planned in the same format as the music lessons and the teacher played some of the music to help the pupils remember what they had done.

LESSON 2 MUSIC – follow up	30 September	25 minutes	PUPILS: SG, SP

AIMS
1. To recall items from music lesson of previous Friday
2. To express an opinion for the type of activities experienced
3. To draw and write about one aspect

RESOURCES
1. Tape recorder and music from last lesson
2. Picture sheets for prompts
3. Paper, pencils, crayons

VOCABULARY
loud noisy quiet music
sad happy
Body part names
like/don't like sing
dance instrument listen
pencil felt tip crayon
colour name
At pupil's direction

CONTENT
1. Play tapped songs and introductory music from last lesson to remind pupils of what we did
2. Decide what pictures represent and discuss
3. Draw a picture of an aspect of the music lesson
4. Pupil to dictate sentence then copy-write

LANGUAGE
Ask what they remember. Encourage 2-word utterance from both
Identify objects, express an opinion
Talk about what pupil wishes to draw, choose medium, name colour
Pupils to state key words, be given other words to complete sentence

EVALUATION
Consider use of tape recorder to record utterances next time
S and S both remembered activities, SG – good recall of sequence of events
Expressed preferences and recorded on sheet
Decided on drawings and were both clear about what they wanted to do
Vocabulary – named body parts, including adjective and noun for eyes, knees, etc. but this could be rote repetition from memory of 'Body' song
Described music appropriately – loud/quiet
Repeat this session at the end of the module
Need to be clear about what I want to record and assess

Figure 9.4

The boys had good recall. They were clear about their activities and tried to express their particular interests. They copy-wrote a single sentence and drew a picture which clearly referred to the music lesson. On reflection, the teacher thought that for her own benefit it would have been useful to have taped this lesson in order to have a precise record of vocabulary and language used. (Figure 9.4 contains the planning and pupil work for this lesson.)

The intention was also to follow the seventh lesson at the end of the module with another session for Steve and Sam. The lesson was planned as before and the teacher intended to assess the pupils' learning with particular reference to vocabulary acquisition, recall, self-evaluation and the ability to make a negative statement when asked to express a preference. Sam was absent for both Lesson 7 and this follow up. The tape recorder did not record on this occasion and although the teacher noted some of Steve's achievements and he completed his written and pictorial work, some of the detail was lost. The boys repeated this lesson on Sam's return to school. This time a recording and a transcription were made. However, it had been more than two weeks since Sam had been in a music lesson and the teacher had to constantly ask leading questions and give prompts. The activity suggested that Sam had difficulty with detailed recall of events, although he had retained some new vocabulary. Also, in the planning of this second follow up, the teacher had tried to include some of the speech sound work set by the speech and language therapist. This was very difficult to incorporate alongside the other aims and the lesson seemed to become too contrived. It would be important to discuss this with the therapist so that therapy activities could be planned which could be integrated into lessons and perhaps some work would have to be undertaken by the therapist individually with the child. The teacher concluded that her own aims had been rather unrealistic and that they must be revised for future lessons. The checklist pro forma (Figure 9.5) was useful as a summary record of some of the language elements and this could be developed to record more systematically the progress made against the aims for the lessons or for individuals. It would have been more appropriate for any written work to be undertaken at the time of the music lesson so that it could be directly linked with the pupil's experience. At this time contextual clues are available so that conditions are more likely to elicit spontaneous language than an artificial re-creation at a later date.

Pictorial evaluation sheets were designed for the pupils. These were used at the beginning of the module for discussion purposes and at the end for the pupils to make a final self-evaluation and to stick on sad or happy faces to reflect their own judgement on their reaction. As this was a new approach in music, at first the pupils merely indicated whether they liked or disliked a particular activity. However, by the end of the module most were able to express an opinion on their own performance for at least two of the activities. The teacher planned to develop symbolic evaluation sheets further following this module.

146

CHECKLIST		
Date	**Comments** 21.11.96 SG	18.11.96 SP
Recall of own experience	'sing' 'dance' SG found this difficult – too long an absence from last music lesson – but remembered home experience	'Dancing' 'Listening' 'Clap your hands' 'Singing'
self-evaluation	SG pointed to pictures for easy/hard in response to questions	
Negative statement	'not good' – in response to a choice question	Only in response to a modelled answer
Vocabulary loud/noisy quiet sad happy	'loud' 'ssh' 'sad face' 'hap face'	'loud' 'quiet' √ √
colours brown blue green grey red ginger white brown black	x repeated after SP gave answer repeated after SP gave answer x √ x x 'grey' √	x √ √ x √ x √ √ √
body parts feet toes knees hands eyes lips	√ 'elbow' √ √ 'tongue'	√ √ √ √ √ √
family names brother sister uncle grandma grandad baby	(In response to photographs) √ √ x √ x (S does not have a grandad) √	(In response to photographs) √ √ √ √ √ √

Figure 9.5

The activities had followed a regular pattern each week. Experience suggested that establishing a predictable order to the lessons helped the pupils to concentrate on improving their skills and performance in small steps within a familiar routine. In the evaluation of the final lesson, the teacher returned to the original aims and considered how far these had been achieved. Below is the lesson content and evaluation for Lesson 7.

Lesson 7

Aim 1: To be able to recognise loud and quiet music.

All pupils demonstrated some understanding of the concepts of loudness and quietness; they now used the words confidently and made choices about which type of music they wished to hear. Michael showed awareness by his body actions, stilling for the quiet music and becoming more restless with the louder music.

Aim 2: To clap rhythms to words which name body parts.

Ruth, Darren – can clap 4-beat rhythm.
Sam, Polly – can clap 3-beat rhythm.
Richard, Michael – will occasionally clap to music or word chants but not in a regular pattern.
All pupils can name familiar body parts and Michael can indicate feet and hands.

Aim 3: To respond vocally to symbols for happy and sad as a chant.

All except Michael understood the sad and happy symbols; as a group and as individuals all could respond to a series of symbols.

Aim 4: To sing and sign two songs.

All pupils enjoyed the taped songs; most could join in some of the phrases of the choruses and Polly and Darren could also sing some of the verses. Polly, Steve and Sam particularly enjoyed dancing to the music, but this needs to be considered for future lessons as this then inhibits their ability to sing at the same time.

Aim 5: To experiment with untuned percussion and tuned notes which contrast high and low.

All the pupils enjoyed their work with the range of musical instruments. In particular, Sam showed considerable sensitivity when working with a xylophone. He played high notes to indicate happiness and low notes to indicate sadness and he gave a simple explanation of what he was doing.

The concept of high and low notes was not explored in any depth, as the pupils seemed to find it too difficult to understand. The words 'high' and 'low' have other meanings than those associated with sound (linked with height) which may make them particularly difficult for these children. This is something which can be returned to in future lessons, perhaps when the pupils have had more experience. However, symbols were introduced to indicate loudness and quietness and the pupils enjoyed 'conducting' the rest of the group. The group generally showed considerable control in trying to respond quickly to a given signal. It might be useful to extend this with diminuendo and crescendo symbols for the next module.

Aim 6: To record some work on tape and for pupils to evaluate it.

Once the technical problems of the tape recorder had been resolved, the pupils seemed to really enjoy this part of the lessons. Polly, Darren and Ruth all managed to operate the tape recorder independently once they had been shown how. This activity proved the best language stimulus. The pupils commented on whether the music they had played was loud or quiet and whether or not they liked the sound they had created. Darren and Polly were able to make evaluative comments on their own performance.

Darren: I was good there, I played it right.
Polly: It's good, I can play with that [xylophone and beater].

The pupils all used the pictorial evaluation sheets and, with support from the teacher and support assistants, they were able to indicate which areas of activity they were good at and which they found more difficult. MG was able to express a preference for an activity by choosing the Walkman from a choice of two symbol cards. Opportunities for these pupils to express opinions and take more control of their activities is often limited and it is important to consider these as aims in lessons.

- Writing specific language targets into lesson plans ensured that the development of language was linked with the context and was associated with all curriculum areas. It created opportunities for the pupils to develop the ability to make choices and to express opinions. It was useful to focus on particular vocabulary, which extended the repertoire of most of the pupils. The repetition helped the children to extend their understanding by

149

increasing the opportunities for use of the vocabulary in a range of subjects.

- The teacher and the speech and language therapist decided to develop a prompt sheet which should enable class teachers to focus more closely on both vocabulary and general language functions when planning their lessons.
- The learning support staff commented that it was very helpful to have clear written aims and lesson notes prior to the lesson so that they could be more fully involved.
- The music lessons met the requirements of the National Curriculum as all areas of musical development were addressed at some point during the module. Individual needs were also addressed for both music and language. A particular success was the development of a communications board for Michael following the choices he initially made from simple pictures during the music lesson.
- Although Sam and Steve did what was required for the written work, the teacher was the least satisfied with the organisation for this part. This would be reconsidered for the next module and perhaps incorporated for more pupils at the end of the module as part of the pupil evaluation process.
- The pupils' self-evaluation was very successful. The children began to be aware that they could express opinions on their own and others' performance and some pupils were beginning to be able to justify those opinions.

Conclusion

The cyclical process of planning, doing, reflecting and then making adjustments based on experience was very useful. It led to increased communication between staff with a consequent sharing of information and observations. This resulted not only in the development of ideas for teaching and learning but in staff feeling that they could support each other in their practice.

Chapter 10

Language and learning in Mathematics

Introduction

This chapter outlines and discusses the planning, teaching and assessment of an area of the curriculum to a group of children who attend a language unit, functionally integrated into a special school for children with moderate learning difficulties. The Unit currently caters for eight children ranging in age from 7 to 11 years. They have a range of difficulties, including difficulties in understanding, phonology, word-finding and semantics, pragmatics and using language appropriately, as well as associated perceptual and fine motor coordination. Many have difficulties in developing literacy skills. The Unit is staffed by a teacher, a qualified nursery nurse and a full-time speech and language therapist. The children spend each morning in the language unit where emphasis is on the core areas of the curriculum and individual speech and language programmes. In the afternoon the children are integrated into their peer classes in the main school where they access the foundation subjects and benefit from social integration. There is close liaison between unit staff and the class teachers to ensure continuity and progression of teaching and speech and language objectives.

The chapter discusses the planning, teaching and assessment of a specific area of the mathematics curriculum. There are three main sections. Firstly, an overview of the planning and assessment process in the school is outlined and provides a context for the planning pro forma developed by the teacher. Secondly, a discussion of a completed pro forma shows detailed planning, demonstrating how both learning difficulties and speech and language needs of the individuals have influenced differentiation. The importance of how the use of resources, classroom organisation and input from other professionals influences the planning process is also discussed. Finally, a discussion of the teaching and assessment of the activities leads to a critical evaluation of the whole process. Conclusions identify what was successful and what could be further improved.

An overview of the planning and assessment process

Since the 1988 Education Reform Act it has been every pupil's entitlement to:

> Share the right to a broad and balanced curriculum, including the National Curriculum. (National Curriculum Council 1989b, p. 1)

Having this right is one thing but being able to access such a curriculum and make progress within it is quite another. Children with speech and language difficulties require carefully planned and differentiated work which takes into account their particular problems (Martin and Miller 1996). Indeed, the National Curriculum Council (1989b) states:

> Curriculum development plans, schemes of work, and classroom and school environments need to be closely aligned with the teaching and needs and individual curriculum plans of pupils with learning difficulties and disabilities so that maximum access to the National Curriculum is ensured. (p. 7)

It is this statement which guides the curriculum planning of the school here. The school has devised a learning policy which states that:

> curriculum provision is directed by the explicit aim of creating an enriched learning environment characterised by challenge, stimulation and structure. Such an environment sets out to foster each child's cognitive, physical, emotional and social development.

This statement places the child at the centre of the learning process and stresses an individual approach to planning and assessment. Explicit also within this learning policy is a recognition of how children learn. Bruner's (1981) work on representation which shows how children organise and make sense of the world has influenced much of this policy. As a result planning must focus on matching the task to the learner's knowledge, ability and interest, encourage activity based on learning and be cross-curricular wherever possible.

Given these guiding principles set out in the learning policy, planning throughout the school is divided into two areas. Firstly, all children have an Individual Education Plan covering the core areas of English and Mathematics. These plans take into account the child's individual needs and allows for many basic skills to be continually reinforced. An example of an individual core curriculum plan is shown as Figure 10.1.

The second area of planning is cross-curricular. This ensures that the core skills are reinforced in a variety of contexts to ensure opportunities for generalisation. All staff have been involved in the planning of cross-curricular topics and themes to ensure continuity and progression throughout the years Reception to Year 6. The language unit topic for the autumn term was 'Houses and Homes' with planning sheets similar to those shown in Figure 10.2.

	Core Curriculum				
Name:				**Date:**	
Time span	Curriculum Area	Objectives	Materials/ Activities	Observation	Level
Autumn term	English: speaking listening reading writing	e.g. to increase appropriate participation in conversation	e.g. Newstime; conversations in class with adults/peers		
	Maths: Number AT2 Measure AT3 Money	e.g. rote count to 10 recognise numbers to 5	e.g. children's names number songs worksheets		
	Collecting, recording, processing data AT4	e.g. to sequence days of the week	e.g. daily routine; today, yesterday, tomorrow		

Figure 10.1: An example of an individual core curriculum plan

English:	stories, poems, sequencing, role play	**Science:**	materials: wood, glass electricity forces
	HOUSES AND HOMES		
Maths:	number recognition number bands – 0–10 Money	**Technology:**	making houses I.T: Albert's House Teddy Bear's Post

Figure 10.2 Example of a topic for 'Houses and Homes'

Assessment both at the core and cross-curricular level is ongoing and comments can be added to the observation sections at any time. These observations and comments build to form the basis of the child's annual review report to parents. They also help the teacher to assess the child's achievement within the National Curriculum which is recorded on profile sheets. These profile sheets contain a list of statements of attainment as set out in the Level Descriptions for each National Curriculum subject. Progress is recorded as follows – '√' area has been visited, '**x**' progress is being made, '•' attainment has been reached. An example of a profile sheet for mathematics is shown in Figure 10.3.

Attainment Target 1: Using and applying mathematics
Level 1
(a)   use mathematics as an integral part of classroom activities
(b)   use materials provided for a task
(c)   represent work with objects or picutres
(d)   talk about own work and ask questions
(e)   rcognise simple patterns based on experience
(f)   recognise simple relationships based on experience

Figure 10.3 An example of a profile sheet for Level 1 Maths

Recently, the school has developed these profiles to include attainment whilst working towards Level 1. It was felt that whilst many children found attaining Level 1 a very slow process they were making very good progress towards this target and as such their success should be recorded. As Miller (1996) points out:

> One of the important considerations in developing effective assessment and record keeping systems is the need to ensure scope for celebrating progress over time as well as attainment at a given moment. (p. 48)

An example of a working towards Level 1 profile for mathematics, Shape, Space and Measure, is shown as Figure 10.4.

Within this framework of whole-school planning and assessment individual teachers are free to develop their own methods of short-term daily and weekly planning and assessment. Figure 10.5 shows a completed pro forma designed to help manage this short-term planning, teaching and assessment. It can be used for any subject or topic but in this instance deals with a specific area of the mathematics curriculum.

Maths: Shape, Space and Measure
Working towards Level 1

1. Can match objects to another by shape – square
2. Can match objects to another by shape – rectangle
3. Can match objects to another by shape – triangle
4. Can match objects to another by shape – circle
5. Can sort objects by shape – square
6. Can sort objects by shape – rectangle
7. Can sort objects by shape – triangle
8. Can sort objects by shape – circle

Figure 10.4 Part of working towards Level 1 Maths: Shape, Space and Measure

Names	Short-term objectives	Links with Speech/Language objectives	Comments	Next Step
MO	Describe people/objects	To develop correct use of personal pronouns	GA: good, no problems with activities	GA: to be introduced to more comparatives
GA	tall/short			
GM	tallest/shortest			
EW	taller/shorter			
JH				
MR				
CH	to consolidate			
RJ	use of big/little			

Figure 10.5 Lesson plans

Planning

Long- and short-term targets

As can be seen from the planning pro forma targets were identified as long- and short-term aims and objectives. The long-term aims were taken from the National Curriculum Level Descriptions (Department of Education 1995a) which outline the level of attainment necessary for achievement at any particular level. The short-term objectives are a breakdown of the steps leading to this level of attainment.

It had already been recorded on the individual core curriculum plans that all the children would undertake work on 'measure' during the autumn term. The teacher then looked at the individual targets for each child and recorded them on to the planning sheet under the heading 'Short-term objectives'. The targets varied depending on the child's level of ability. For example, the teacher felt that CH and RJ had less experience and knowledge of the concepts being studied and it would be unrealistic for them to achieve the targets set for the other children. Likewise the targets set for use of numbers again depended on the child's knowledge and ability, some were able to work with numbers to 20 whilst others concentrated on numbers to 5.

How these targets were to be achieved, that is, the specific tasks and activities, are outlined in the lesson plans shown in Figure 10.5. They are discussed after another aspect of the planning process has been considered, namely the links with speech and language objectives.

Links with speech and language objectives

When devising the planning pro forma unit staff all agreed on the importance of including this section given that it is hard to keep separate the demands of the

155

curriculum and the speech and language needs of the children (Armstrong *et al.* 1995). These are interrelated in several ways, as outlined below.

Firstly, the vocabulary demanded by the curriculum can be problematic for children who find retaining, recalling and generalising new vocabulary difficult. In this case it was important for the new vocabulary *tall, short, short, shorter, taller, tallest* and *smallest* to be understood, used correctly and generalised if the mathematical concept of comparatives was to be fully mastered. The teacher and the speech and language therapist decided that, as well as planning activities which focused on the development and use of such vocabulary, other strategies such as clapping out the syllabic beat of the word and using Makaton signs (Walker 1976) and symbols (Walker 1985) would also be used. When and for which children these strategies were to be used can be seen in the lesson plans.

The speech and language therapist also decided to link comparative vocabulary into ongoing comprehension work based on the Derbyshire Language Scheme (Knowles and Masidlover 1982). This was a good opportunity to directly link more structured language activities with the vocabulary and comprehension demands of the curriculum in the classroom. Furthermore, by comparing observations in both settings the teacher and the speech and language therapist would have a fuller picture of the children's ability to demonstrate understanding and the correct use of the new vocabulary in a range of contexts.

The unit staff also agreed that Activity 1, which was for the children to draw around each other, working in pairs, with collage and paint, in the lesson plans in Figure 10.5 was a good opportunity to provide a different context for reviewing the vocabulary associated with body parts and clothing focused on during a topic on 'Ourselves' earlier in the year.

The speech and language difficulties of the children also need to be considered in relation to the demands of the tasks and activities required by the curriculum (Armstrong *et al.* 1995). The lesson plans show that the children were expected to perform a range of 'generic activities' (Alexander 1992) including writing, use of apparatus, reading, listening and looking, drawing and painting, collaborative activities with other children, talking with the teacher and construction. These activities are challenging for pupils with speech and language difficulties.

Careful planning of these activities was necessary, taking into account the speech and language difficulties of individual children. For example, poor short-term auditory memory means MR has difficulty with word-finding, comprehension and literacy activities. The use of signs and symbols and syllable clapping would help him with writing, reading, listening and looking activities. For GM and CH, who have phonological problems, symbols and signing would give them confidence to express themselves during activities which demanded talking with the teacher and collaborative activities with other children. EM has pragmatic problems and difficulties with listening and attention and as a result needs much adult modelling and prompts when completing structured activities. Consequently provision was made in the classroom organisation for her to complete Activities 3, 4 and 5 in the lesson plans on a one-to-one basis with the teacher.

As well as allowing the children to succeed, this careful planning ensures that difficulties with the learning task itself are identified and are not confused with difficulties in communication (SEAC 1990).

The unit staff were also very much aware that their own use of language, their expectations, and the context of the activities would all have an effect on the children's performance. Monitoring their own use of language was essential if we accept Webster and McConnell's (1987) view that:

> instead of seeing language difficulties as residing wholly within the child, attention is focused on the patterns of interaction between child and others. (p. 154)

Finally, it is important to consider that curriculum activities can be an effective vehicle for teaching particular speech and language skills (Armstrong *et al.* 1995). The unit staff looked closely at the objectives outlined by the speech and language therapist to see where they could specifically be taught in classroom activities. Three aspects were identified: using personal pronouns, 'who?' questions, and turn-taking skills. Throughout Activities 1, 2 and 3 in the lesson plans the teacher and the nursery nurse were aware of maximising the opportunities to model and teach correct use of personal pronouns such as *I, he, she*. They were also aware of monitoring responses to 'who?' questions, e.g. 'who is the tallest', and noting any spontaneous use of 'who?' questions in the correct context. Activities 1, 2 and 4 demanded collaboration between the children and provided ideal opportunities for developing turn-taking skills.

In planning it was not specifically noted that there would be work on any phonological or grammatical targets. Often the classroom is not the most appropriate context for correcting errors, because correction is outside the communication and cuts across learning (Daines *et al*, 1996). However, the teacher noted in the comments section of the first page of the planning pro forma that JH spontaneously identified the final 't' in *shortest* and *tallest*, a sound he was working on with the speech and language therapist. This spontaneous comment led the teacher to naturally focus on this sound with the rest of the group and provided an excellent opportunity to teach some phonology. The teacher was also able to pass on the information to the speech and language therapist who was delighted that JH had begun to generalise specific speech sound work into other contexts.

In order for this kind of collaborative work to be successful, the teacher and speech and language therapist recognised the importance of allowing time for joint planning. In this particular setting the speech and language therapist is fortunate in being employed by the education authority and works full-time in the language unit. Hence, there is not the same pressure of time that research by Evans and Jowett (1996) found to be the main cause of frustration between many teachers and therapists. Nevertheless even in this enviable setting, negotiations with a senior management colleague were necessary to ensure adequate liaison time.

Once the long- and short-term targets had been planned and integrated with the speech and language objectives it was then necessary to plan how these were to be taught. It was logged on the lesson plans outlined in Figure 10.5.

Lesson Plans

These lesson plans outline the tasks and activities the children do, the personnel involved and the materials and resources used. This has implications for both classroom organisation and differentiation.

The language unit is organised on an integrated day where the children can complete a range of activities in any one session. This allows for flexible class and group organisation. The lesson plans provide details of activities which can be incorporated into an integrated day rather than showing the full content of a lesson. For example the initial drawing and collaging work took a week for the nursery nurse to complete, working with one or two children each morning. On the other hand Activity 2, asking the children to predict *tallest/shortest* and to sequence pictures in pairs, took a whole class lesson involving all staff.

Moreover, an integrated morning also means staff can be used flexibly. The language unit is fortunate in having three adults available which means that the range and quality of supported learning can be increased (Armstrong *et al.* 1995). For example, EW was able to benefit from one-to-one support from the teacher in Activities 3, 4 and 5.

The lesson plans also outline how work is differentiated. This may take different forms, e.g. language of instruction, resources, teacher focus, grouping/organisation, outcome, task. Some examples of differentiation have already been given above when looking at target setting and the links between speech and language needs and the curriculum. Others can be given now, e.g. GA requires the use of a non-slip mat for writing activities in Activities 3, 4 and 5, whilst JH and EW require the use of plastic numbers in order to complete Activity 4.

Lessons were planned to cover 5 sessions under the heading of Proposed Lesson Plans. However as suggested in Chapter 2, the development of suitable teaching and learning activities must be based on a staged process and must always be open to change in the light of experience and new information. For this reason the section Modified Lesson Plans (Figure 10.6) was added to allow for changes as the children worked through the series of activities. At this point assessment and planning are very much interrelated. This is very important if we accept the view that any assessment framework should place assessment as

Proposed Lesson Plans			Comments	Modified Lesson Plans		
Activity 5	*Who*	*Materials*		*Activity*	*Who*	*Materials*
Complete worksheets	MO	Worksheet	MO, GA – no problem	Prepare	JH	Lego
	MR	Pencils	GM, MR – independent, need signs	other ways	GA	
	GA	Non-slip mat	JH needed help reading	of recording	EW	
	JH		EW: 1:1 support	data	GM with teacher	
	GM/teacher					
	EW with N					

Figure 10.6 An example of part of a section of the Modified Lesson Plans

159

integral to the teaching and learning process (McCarthy 1990). It is therefore unhelpful to divide planning and assessment into distinct headings. Nevertheless so that a critical evaluation of the planning and subsequent teaching sessions can be made, teaching and assessment are discussed separately.

Teaching and assessment

All the activities were completed by the children and most were successful. However the comments relating to Activity 4 in the lesson plans in Figure 10.5 illustrate how not all activities went to plan. In this case the teacher had not fully considered the children's ability to record information appropriately. Perceptual difficulties and motor problems meant MO and MR could not accurately draw representations of the Lego bricks and as a result MO's shortest tower was drawn taller than his tallest tower. As these children were the most capable the teacher realised she needed to alter the recording procedure if any of the other children were to succeed. This is shown in the modified lesson plans, Activity 5 in Figure 10.6.

Assessment was ongoing and the comments section of the lesson plans were completed after each lesson. A summary of these comments was then made in the comments section on the first page of the pro forma. This provided the information necessary for the next step section to be completed which shows the next stage of planning for the child. In this way assessment is 'providing both "feedback and feedforward"' (Department of Education and Science/Welsh Office, 1987) and remains integral to the education process.

Assessment was also based on the work that the children produced. Comments were made as to how much help the children required or if they completed that task independently. Summative assessments could now be made on the core curriculum sheets and symbols added to the profile sheets. Figure 10.7 shows a 'working towards Level 1' profile sheet for JH with the relevant targets completed.

Assessment of the children's performance also influenced the speech and language intervention targets. In the pro–forma in Figure 10.5, in the 'Next Step' section, the teacher would also note the speech/language targets for the children. For example, after one lesson the teacher noted for the children MO and JH: 'Speech therapist to review personal pronouns'.

Critical evaluation

Overall, the planning, teaching and assessment of this area of the curriculum was successful. During the activities all the children made progress and developed

Maths: Shape, Space and Measure
Working towards Level 1: for JH

33. Can compare objects for size ✔
34. Can sort objects by size
35. Can describe objects in terms of their measurement – tall ✔
36. Can describe objects in terms of their measurement – short ✔
37. Can describe objects in terms of their measurement – long ✔
38. Can describe objects in terms of their measurement – thick
39. Can describe objects in terms of their measurement – thin
40. Can describe objects in terms of their measurement – high
41. Can describe objects in terms of their measurement – low
42. Is able to compare lengths to find the longest object
43. Is able to compare lengths to find the longest object
44. Is able to compare lengths to find the longest object ✗
45. Is able to compare lengths to find the longest object ✗

Figure 10.7 Working towards Level 1 Maths: Shape, Space and Measure Attainment. Target 3 for JH showing the targets he has completed

their knowledge and skills. However it was felt that some children, for example MO and GA, could have been challenged more and would have coped with the inclusion of more comparatives such as *long/short, thick/thin*. For other children such as RJ and CH many more experiences will need to be provided before meaningful awareness of comparative vocabulary is developed. The overall success of the structured activities cannot be measured until the children are seen to generalise and apply their knowledge in a variety of contexts. The unit staff will continue to monitor this success and opportunities for further assessment will be made during the next topic, 'Things on Wheels', in the spring term.

The unit staff found the planning pro forma a useful addition to the existing planning sheets. The teacher felt however that the comments section of page 1 of the pro forma, which provided a summary of the comments made in the lesson plans, was an unnecessary addition. It was decided that in future the summary contents were to be made directly on to the core curriculum sheets.

Most importantly the unit staff agreed that the planning pro forma allowed for greater collaboration when planning both curriculum and speech and language targets. In the existing planning there was no real facility for these two areas to be planned together. As a result much of the previous collaboration had been informal with general areas rather than specific objectives being discussed. The layout of the pro forma now meant that both curriculum objectives and speech and language targets could be combined. This was done successfully in this instance and the unit staff are optimistic that continued collaboration will be reflected in the progress made by children.

References

Adams, C., Byers Brown, B. and Edwards, M. (1997) *Developmental Disorders of Language,* 2nd edn. London: Whurr.

Alexander, R. (1992) *Policy and Practice in Primary Education.* London: Routledge.

Andersen-Wood, L. and Smith, B. R. (1997) *Working With Pragmatics.* Bicester: Winslow Press.

Armstrong, A., Daines, B., Halliday, P. and Wright, J. (1995) *Models of Management.* SEEP 39, Text 1, Distance Education Course: Speech and Language Difficulties. School of Education, The University of Birmingham, UK.

Barrs, M., Ellis, S., Hester, H. and Thomas, A. (1988) *The Primary Language Record.* London: Centre for Language in Primary Education.

Bates, E. (1976) *Language in Context: The Acquisition of Pragmatics.* New York: Academic Press.

Bates, V., Coyle, D., Laverick, C. (1996) *The Special Schools Dimension: A distance learning resource for teacher of MFL in Special Schools.* London: Centre for Information on Language Teaching and Research.

Bishop, D. V. M. and Mogford, K. (1988) *Language Development in Exceptional Circumstances.* Edinburgh: Churchill Livingstone.

Bloom, B. S. and Krathwohl, D. R. (1965) *The Taxonomy of Educational Objectives, the Classification of Educational Goals. Handbook 1: Cognitive Domain.* New York: McKay.

Brown, R. (1973) *A First Language: The Early Stages.* Cambridge, Mass.: Harvard University Press.

Bruner, J. (1981) 'What is representation?' in Roberts, M. and Tamburrim, J. (eds) *Child Development 0–5.* Edinburgh: Holmes McDougall.

Bulman, L. (1985) *Teaching Language and Study Skills in Secondary Science.* London: Heinemann.

Carr, W and Kemmis, S. (1986) *Becoming Critical: education, knowledge and action research.* Lewes: Falmer Press.

Cromer, R. F. (1991) *Language and Thought in Normal and Handicapped Children.* Oxford: Blackwell.

Crystal, D. (1987) *Child Language, Learning and Linguistics,* 2nd edn. London: Edward Arnold.

Crystal, D. and Varley, R. (1993) *An Introduction to Language Pathology,* 3rd edn. London: Whurr.

Cummins, J. (1984) *Bilingualism and Special Education: Issues in Assessment and Pedagogy.* Clevedon: Multilingual Matters.

Daines, B., Fleming, P., Miller, C. (1996) *Spotlight on Special Education Needs: Speech and language difficulties.* Tamworth, Staffs: NASEN.

Deane, M. (1992) 'Teaching MFL to pupils with special needs? With pleasure!', *Language Learning Journal* **6**, 43–47.

Department for Education and Employment (1995a) *Key Stages One and Two of the National Curriculum.* London: HMSO.

Department for Education and Employment (1995b) *Science in the National Curriculum.* London: HMSO.

Department of Education and Employment (1995c) *Mathematics in the National Curriculum.* London: HMSO.

Department for Education and Employment (1995d) *Modern Foreign Languages in the National Curriculum.* London: HMSO.

Department of Education and Science. (1989) *From Policy to Practice.* London: DES.

Department of Education and Science/Welsh Office (1990) *Modern Foreign Languages for Ages 11 to 16.* London: HMSO.

Department of Education and Science/Welsh Office (1987) *TGAT Report – National Curriculum Task Group on Assessment and Testing.* London: HMSO.

Derbyshire Advisory and Inspection Service (1995) *Key Stage 1 Music Scheme.* Derbyshire Education Authority.

Dockrell, J. and McShane, J. (1993) *Children's Learning Difficulties: a cognitive approach.* Oxford: Blackwell

Ellis, A. and Young, A. (1988) *Human Cognitive Neuropsychology.* Hove: Lawrence Erlbaum Associates.

Evans, C. and Jowett, S. (1996) *Speech and Language Therapy Services for Children.* Slough: NFER.

Feuerstein, R., Rand, Y., Hoffman, M. and Miller, R. (1980) *Instrumental Enrichment.* Glenview, Ill.: Scott Foresman.

Fodor, J. (1983) *The Modularity of Mind.* Cambridge, Mass.: MIT Press.

Foster, S. (1990) *The Communicative Competence of Young Children.* New York: Longman.

Graddol, D., Cheshire, J., Swann, J. (1994) *Describing Language,* 2nd edn. Milton Keynes: Open University.

Gravelle, M. (1996) *Supporting Bilingual Learners in School.* Stoke: Trentham Books.

Harrison, P., Boden, J., Hartley, K. (1992) *Folens Science in Action: Planning and Practice.* London: Folens.

Howell, J. and Dean, E. (1994) *Treating phonological disorders in children: Metaphon – theory into Practice.* London: Whurr.

Jackson, H. (1990) *Grammar and Meaning.* London: Longman.

Jarvis P. (1983) *Professional Education.* Beckenham, Kent: Croom Helm.

Knowles, W. and Masidlover, M. (1982) *Derbyshire Language Scheme.* Derbyshire County Council.

Krashen, S. (1982) *Principles and Practice in Second Language Acquisition.* Oxford: Pergamon.

Kyriacou, C., Benmansour, N., Low, G. (1996) 'Pupil learning styles and foreign language learning'. *Language Learning Journal* **13**, 22–24

Lee, B. (1991) *Extending opportunities: modern foreign languages for pupils with special educational needs.* Slough: National Foundation for Educational Research.

Lenneberg, E. H. (1967) *Biological Foundations of Language.* New York: Wiley.

Mackay, F. (1996) *Essentials for Science. Electricity and magnetism. Key Stage One.* London: Scholastic.

Marshman, A. (In Press) *Teachers' use of non-literal language.* London: The Teacher Training Agency.

Martin, D. and Miller, C. (1996) *Speech and Language Difficulties in the Classroom.* London: David Fulton Publishers.

McCarthy, M. (1990) 'A framework for assessment', *Language and Learning* **4**.

McCartney, E. and Van der Gaag, A. (1996) 'How shall we be judged? Speech and Language therapists in educational settings', *Child Language Teaching and Therapy* (3) **12**, 31–37.

McTear, M. (1985) *Children's Conversations.* Oxford: Blackwell.

Morgan, N., and Saxton, J. (1991) *Teaching, Questioning and Learning.* London: Routledge.

National Curriculum Council (1989a) *Non-Statutory Guidance: Science.* York: NCC.

National Curriculum Council (1989b) *Curriculum Guidance 2: A Curriculum For All.* York: NCC.

National Curriculum Council (1990a) *Curriculum Guidance 2: A Curriculum For All.* London: HMSO.

National Curriculum Council (1990b) *Curriculum Guidance 3: The Whole Curriculum.* York: NCC.

National Curriculum Council (1992a) *Non-Statutory Guidance: Modern Foreign Languages.* London: HMSO.

National Curriculum Council (1992b) *Music in the National Curriculum.* London: HMSO.

Nowicki, S. and Marshall P. Duke (1992) *Helping the child who doesn't fit in.* Atlanta, Ga.: Peachtree Publishers.

Pembry, M. (1992) 'Genetics and language disorder', in Fletcher, P. and Hall, D. (eds) *Specific Speech and Language Disorders in Children.* London: Whurr.

Pinker, S. (1994) *The Language Instinct.* Harmondsworth: Penguin.

Richards, B. (1995) 'Child-directed speech and influences on language acquisition: methodology and inerpretation', in Gallaway, C. and Richards, B. (eds) *Input and Interaction in Language Acquisition, 74–106.* Cambridge: Cambridge University Press.

Rinaldi, W. (1995) *The Social Use of Language Priogramme.* San Francisco: Jossey-Bass.

Rogoff, B. and Wertsch, J. V. (Eds) (1984) 'Children's learning in the "zone of proximal development"', *New Directions for Child Development* **23**.

Royal College of Speech and Language Therapists (1996) *Communicating Quality: professional standards for speech and language therapists*, 2nd edn. London: RCSLT.

Rylands, L. (1974) *The Butterfly.* Burke Books.

Schon, D. (1983) *The reflective practitioner.* London: Temple Smith.

School Curriculum and Assessment Authority (1997) *Use of Language: a common approach.* London: SCAA.

School Examinations and Assessment Council (SEAC) (1990) *A Guide to Teacher Assessment Pack C: A Source book of Teacher Assessment.* London: SEAC.

Skehan, P. (1998) *A Cognitive Approach to Language Learning.* Oxford: Oxford University Press.

Smith, B. R. and Leinonen, E. (1992) *Clinical Pragmatics.* London: Chapman and Hall.

Stackhouse, J. and Wells, B. (1997) *Children's speech and literacy difficulties.* London: Whurr.

Stenhouse, L. (1975) *An introduction to curriculum research and development.* London: Heinemann.

Van der Lely, H. K. J. (1997) 'Language and cognitive development in a grammatical SLI boy: modularity and innatenes, *Journal of Neurolinguistics* **10**, 75–107.

Veliante, N. (1995) 'Teaching languages to pupils with special educational needs: success with pupils with Asperger's Syndrome', in *Languages and Special Educational Needs.* London: Centre for Information on Language Teaching and Research.

Vygotsky, L. S. (1962) *Thought and Language.* Cambridge, Mass.: MIT Press.

Walker, M. (1976) *Line Drawings for the Revised Makaton Vocabulary.* Surrey: MVDP.

Walker, M. (1985) *Symbols for Makaton.* Surrey: MVDP.

Webster, A. and McConnell, C. (1987) *Special Needs in Ordinary Schools. Children with Speech and Language Difficulties.* London: Cassell.

Wells, G. (1985) *Language Development in the Pre-school Years.* Cambridge: Cambridge University Press.

Wheal, R. (1995) 'Unleashing individual potential: a team approach', *Support for Learning* **10** (2), 83–87

Womack, D. (1988) *Special Needs in Ordinary Schools.* London: Cassell Educational Ltd.

Published materials used for teaching

'Watch' series produced by BBC at the request of the Educational Broadcasting Council. Teachers notes and video recording of Programme 7, Spring 1988.

Viewtech 'Where does the rain go after it falls?'. Viewtech Film and Video, Bristol.

Author index

Subject index